WORKING TOGETHER

WORKING TOGETHER

Twelve Principles for
Achieving Excellence in
Managing Projects, Teams,
and Organizations

James P. Lewis

McGraw-Hill
New York Chicago San Francisco Lisbon
London Madrid Mexico City Milan
Montreal New Delhi San Juan
Seoul Singapore Sydney Toronto

Library of Congress Cataloging-in-Publication Data

Lewis, James P.
    Project planning, scheduling, and control / by James P. Lewis. — 3rd ed.
    p. cm.
    ISBN 0-07-136050-6
    1. Industrial project management. 2. Scheduling. I. Title.

    HD69.P75 L493 2000
    658.4′04—dc21
                                                    00-058433
                                                    CIP

McGraw-Hill

A Division of The **McGraw·Hill** *Companies*

1 2 3 4 5 6 7 8 9 0 DOC/DOC 0 9 8 7 6 5 4 3 2 1

ISBN 0-07-137951-7

The sponsoring editor for this book was Catherine Dassopoulos and the production supervisor was Clare Stanley. It was set in Palatino by Judy Brown.

Printed and bound by R. R. Donnelley & Sons Company.

McGraw-Hill books are available at special quantity discounts to use as premiums and sales promotions, or for use in corporate training programs. For more information, please write to the Director of Special Sales, McGraw-Hill, Professional Publishing, 2 Penn Plaza, New York, NY 10121-2298. Or contact your local bookstore.

This book is printed on recycled, acid-free paper containing a minimum of 50% recycled de-inked fiber.

There is no future *out there* waiting to be discovered. We will create the future through our actions. We can either *work together* to build a future in which all human beings can thrive and lead productive, peaceful lives, or we can destroy the world by engaging in destructive behavior.

This book is dedicated to my wife,

Lea Ann Lewis

who has been the best practitioner of Working Together that I have known during the 30 years we have been married.

It is also dedicated to those men and women who understand that working together is only possible if we have what Albert Schweitzer called a reverence for life, which is expressed by mutual respect for each other in spite of differences in views and even objectives. If we can remember that we are all more alike than we are different, we will be more tolerant of the differences.

Working Together is not just about business.

It must become a way of life.

Otherwise, there may be no future.

I am grateful to Alan Mulally and Sherry Mizuta for bringing these principles to my attention, and for working together with me to share them with all of you who will read this book.

CONTENTS

Foreword

I have always wanted to contribute to something really important and useful for the people of our world. I found my dreams in aerospace and the Boeing Company.

I was fortunate to contribute to the development of each of Boeing's commercial jet airplanes: the wonderful, world-changing 707, 727, 737, 747, 757, 767, and 777.

I was also fortunate to contribute to the integration of the talented people and valuable assets of Boeing, McDonnell-Douglas, and Rockwell to create our new Boeing Company in 1996.

And most recently, I was fortunate to be asked to lead the turn-around and restoring of Boeing Commercial Airplanes to its global industry leading position.

Our "working together" principles and practices are a key to these contributions...and a result of these contributions. Our most recent business situation may have been the biggest test of our "working together" principles and practices. Let me share our story.

In 1996, Boeing Commercial Airplanes, once again, was focused on doing the best thing for our customers. Our customers needed many new airplanes to replace their noisier, older airplanes. Boeing committed to dramatically increase production on all of our airplanes, improve our entire production system, and develop a number of new airplanes all simultaneously. In hindsight, we tried to do too much! We actually had to stop global production for lack of parts. And we lost a lot of money and put our wonderful company's future at risk. We disappointed our customers, investors, employees, suppliers, friends, families, and ourselves.

I was asked to get us going again. We all pulled together around our "working together" principles and practices...one more time. We agreed on the importance of our work together. We focused on our customers and each other. We developed a plan that included all of us. We made it okay to share everything...what was going well and what was not going well. We listened to each other. We helped each other. We celebrated every airplane delivery with our customers and our team. We enjoyed our progress. And we enjoyed each other. Following two years of intense "working together," we delivered on all of our airplane commitments, regained our operational efficiency, and started to go to work on using our assets more efficiently. And, most importantly, we regained our confidence and accelerated the development of new products and services for our customers.

Our world is changing fast with global market-based economies and connectivity providing tremendous "working together" growth opportunities for all of us.

We hope our "working together" principles and practices contribute in a small way to your life's work. We really all do fly together! Thank you for your contribution!

Alan Mulally
President and CEO, Boeing Commerical Airplanes

Preface

When my editor, Catherine Dassapoulos, first asked me to write this book, it was supposed to be titled something like *The 10 Keys to Success in Managing Projects*. Her call came just days after I had visited with Alan Mulally, president of the Commercial Airplanes Division of Boeing, and he had shared with me a set of principles that guide his thinking on management. I wrote him and asked if I could use his principles to write a book on project management, and he graciously gave me that permission.

As I began formulating the book, however, I remembered something he said to me during our meeting at his office in Renton. "We don't make much of a distinction between project management and general management," he told me. "To us, they are essentially the same." I agree with him. In fact, one of the concerns that I have about project managers is that they sometimes don't think enough like general managers. In addition, there are only two major differences between managing projects and managing in general. One is that project managers pay considerably greater attention to detailed scheduling. The other is that project managers often don't "own" the people who do project work. Otherwise, they are very similar, and you can expect that the same principles would apply to both.

So I decided to broaden the perspective of the book to include managing projects, teams, and organizations. The principles that Alan espouses are indeed applicable to any and all aspects of managing—whether in profit or not-for-profit organizations, and whether in the public or private sector.

Not only that, but Alan Mulally has demonstrated that they work. In his thirty-year career at Boeing, he has held positions that involved work on every major aircraft that Boeing produced. But it was the 777 that figures most prominently in the public's awareness of Alan and that was responsible for my first meeting with him.

Initially, he was chief engineer of the 777 program. Later he became general manager of the job, and in 1986 he was promoted to president of Commercial Airplanes. From the beginning of the program, he espoused most of the principles outlined in this book. One of them—you can't manage a secret—was developed during the program.

Ask anyone at Boeing and they will all tell you that he is passionate about these principles. He lives by them—as well as any human being can. As Benjamin Franklin wrote in his autobiography, he worked his entire lifetime to master a set of principles, with humility being one that forever gave him difficulty.

For Mulally, the principles are so important that he begins his weekly business plan review meeting by reviewing the principles with everyone present—a practice that he started during the 777 program. He also ends the meeting by reviewing them. Why? Because unless you have a coherent, guiding set of principles, you can't develop sound practices. One of his principles is that the data sets you free. I would say that a set of principles also sets you free—free from the fire fighting, grasping for quick fixes, and all the other futile attempts so many managers make to survive the turbulent times in which we live.

Although Alan did not invent all of these guiding rules, he has made them his philosophy of managing, and they have proved their worth. I believe that *authorship* is not nearly as important as *application*.

In the short time since I met Alan Mulally in September 2000, I too have become passionate about these principles. I have already begun to incorporate them into my seminars on project management and fully intend to "spread the gospel," as some might say. I wrote this book because I believe you will also find them effective, and goodness knows we need all the help we can get in improving the management of many organizations.

However, I also believe that these principles are character-based. It takes character to follow them. But to the extent that this is done, we will build character in the people affected by them, and we will transform our organizations into "kinder-gentler" places to work, to use former President Bush's favorite expression.

To sum this up, I not only got to meet with Alan Mulally during my September visit, but I spent about an hour and a half with Captain John Cashman, who is now chief test pilot for Boeing Commercial and who also piloted the 777 on its first flight. The first flight of a new airplane is a momentous occasion, and this particular one is documented in video by Karl Sabbagh in *21st Century Jet,* aired on PBS and available for purchase from them. Even as a late observer of the video, I found myself caught up in the excitement of that moment.

So one of the first things I asked Cashman during our meeting was, "What were you thinking when the plane left the ground?" His response was sober. "Well, you're so engrossed in what you're doing," he said, "that you really don't think about risk. You're just focused on doing your job." That made perfect sense to me.

About an hour later, though, as I was preparing to leave, he said, "You know, I do remember something. When the wheels left the ground, I thought, 'It actually works!'" What a wonderful way to summarize five years of work by thousands of people, scattered throughout forty-four countries and every continent. And to me it applies not only to the engineering of a great airplane, but to the principles that guided the management of the entire program.

I should say before going further that this is a book about the principles. It is not a book about Boeing. There are some very excellent books about the company itself. Also, even though the 777 program first brought me to visit Boeing, this book is not about that program. Sabbagh documented it so thoroughly that there is no need to write more.

I invite you to try these principles. But be persistent in them. You will find that it takes time. Even after a decade of applying them, I know that not everyone at Boeing has bought into them. Nevertheless, for those who are convinced, I know they would join me in saying, like John Cashman, "It actually works!"

Thank you, Alan Mulally, for sharing them with me and with the rest of the world!

Jim Lewis
Vinton, Virginia
November 25, 2000

Acknowledgments

I want to thank my editor, Catherine Dassopoulos, for suggesting the concept for this book and for her enthusiasm for the project as it progressed. I have worked with Catherine on several book projects now, and she has always been a pleasure to work with.

Judy Brown typeset the final text, and as she has done on several of my previous books, her work is impeccable.

As all authors readily acknowledge, no project like this could be successful without help from a lot of people. Alan Mulally and Sherry Mizuta have been key players in this project from the start. Had it not been for their support, the book could not have been written. Given their already heavy workloads, taking on a project like this can only be a labor of love. For that matter, just the sheer volume of correspondence they receive makes it a special honor for me that they took time to work with me and answer my many questions.

A number of Boeing employees have also been of immeasurable help. Ron Ostrowski has initiated several dialogues with me that resulted in significant contributions. Walt Gillette shared his thoughts with me about the power of Alan Mulally's vision for the 777 program. Jim Jamieson took time out of his busy travel schedule to suggest that I address Managing for Value. John Monroe talked with me about building 777s. Rick Gardner, who is in Program Management for Airplane Programs, and Marty Bentroitt, who is in Sales, took time to talk with me face-to-face during a visit to Boeing. John Cashman spent an hour and a half talking with me about flying in a way that conveyed his true love for the job (or should I call it his hobby?). Patrick Shanahan talked with me about managing an assembly group during the early days of the 777 program, and gave me some excellent insight into the way Alan Mulally and Phil Condit work. And retired vice president Peter Morton talked with me by phone early one morning and suggested that I attend one of Mulally's Business Plan Review Meetings to see the principles firsthand. That was a great suggestion and contributed enormously to the book.

Then there were the Boeing drivers who escorted me to a number of venues. I only remember one name—Bruce Jamieson—but thanks to all of them for sharing their love of Boeing with me.

Finally, Kay Sigmund and Linda Merry both bent over backwards to help me make travel and transportation arrangements while I visited Boeing, in addition to forwarding e-mail to Boeing employees when I did not know their addresses.

As usual, my wife, Lea Ann, has put her soul into making the book look like more than dull, printed words. Readers consistently tell me how much they like the art in my books, and the credit all goes to her.

Since Lea Ann is not proficient at the computer, we owe special thanks to Bill Adams, of Adams Graphics, for turning her concepts into finished illustrations. He works with minimal instruction and has now helped with several of our books.

FROM THE MADISON CLASS

While I was working on the book, I taught a class in Madison, Wisconsin, and asked the participants to tell me why each principle was meaningful. They contributed some very useful insight into the principles, and I want to acknowledge their contributions here:

Jeff Augustine, Becky Barry, Mike Barth, Cori Blomdahl, David Burkhart, Josephine Diaz, Gordon Eaken, John Gerritsen, Fred Haynes, Kevin Helle, Kent Huff, Angela Hustad Beutler, George Knezic, David Knudtson, Dean Krueger, Steve Kruisselbrink, Donna Livesey, Kristine Majdacic, Steven Murphy, Robert Nevruz, John O'Connor, Ellen Pedretti, Philip Peichel, Greg Pettigrew, Tyrone Pipkin, Rita Preza, Charles Rounds, Parthasarathy Sabniviss, Eric Sander, Stephanie Sasser, Denise Schaller, Phillip Schultz, Patrick Shanahan (not the same as the one at Boeing), Dennis Sweeney, Todd Toussaint, Terry Troutt, Beth Vissman, and Eric Wagenknecht.

1

First Flight

*O*n Sunday, June 12, 1994, Alan Mulally woke up early. This was the day! He had dreamed of this day for over five years, and finally, here it was—the day when *his* airplane was to be flown for the first time.

The day before, the plane had *almost* been flown. Captain John Cashman and his copilot Ken Higgins made a dash down the runway, reaching a takeoff speed of 140 knots, lifting the nose off the ground, but keeping the plane earthbound—a maneuver to see how the plane handled on the ground before takeoff. However, some observers were sure it *had* left the ground, though Cashman said that instruments indicated "that there was always at least one set of wheels on the ground, and that people were misled when he rocked the plane from side to side to lift each main set in turn off the ground" (Sabbagh, 1996, p. 274). Today they would do more than taxi around on the ground. This time, it would be the real thing.

The weather that day was worse than the day before. "Gray, angry clouds hung over Everett, and gusts of rain swept the tarmac at Paine Field" (op cit., p. 275). If this were prophetic, it was not a good sign. By time for the flight, the weather had improved somewhat, but the wind was still high, so they waited for about forty-five minutes, then gave the go-ahead, even though they still had a 12-knot tailwind.

Fortunately, the weather was not prophetic. All eyes were riveted on the big silver bird as it rolled down the runway, lifted off with the grace of a ballerina, and soared skyward. There were cheers from the crowd, many of whom raised their arms in the air in a show of triumph. For more than 10,000 designers and another 30,000 assemblers, administrators, and numerous people in other professions who had been part of the program, it was *their* airplane and their victory, because they had not just been *involved* in it, they had been *committed* to it.

For Alan Mulally, it was the ultimate professional experience. Seldom does an individual get to direct the engineering of a totally new airplane—for most people, there could be only one chance in a lifetime. Yes, there had been contributions to other airplanes, but this was different. For Alan Mulally was the father of this airplane—if not in the true biological sense, certainly in the metaphorical sense. And so, as the beautiful creature climbed into the clouds, Mulally could not take his eyes off it. He stood with his hands clasped in front of him, appearing awestruck at the sight, almost oblivious to those around him. At one point, he wiped a tear from his right eye. "Didn't you think it was pretty?" he asked Gordon McKinzie of United Airlines, who had also been committed to the program from the beginning. And then *their* 777 disappeared behind the clouds and the moment they had worked so hard for during the past four years was past. The memory, however, would be with them for a lifetime.

In addition to being a tremendous engineering achievement, the success of the 777 was also proof to Mulally that the management principles he had espoused throughout the program were correct. "Working Together" had been a new approach for Boeing, so radically different from their previous practice of designing airplanes that the expression was screened on the nose of that first plane, designated WA001 on Boeing's accounting records.

The general concept of working together was recommended to Phil Condit and Mulally by Don Peterson, then president of Ford. Peterson suggested that Mulally talk with Lew Veraldi, who was managing a project for Ford using a radical approach in which customers, suppliers, and manufacturing were working together with the engineers to produce what would later become one of Ford's most successful products ever—the Taurus. And it was Veraldi who convinced Mulally that this was the right approach to use in managing any large-scale project.

Tom Peters has written that, using this approach, Ford created a car that ". . . won kudos for design and quality—and [came] in under the proposed product development budget by almost one-half *billion* dollars to boot" (Peters, 1987, p. 212).

In describing the project, Lew Veraldi says,

> *With Taurus . . . we brought all disciplines together, and did the whole process simultaneously as well as sequentially. The manufacturing people worked right with the design people, engineering people, sales and purchasing, legal, service, and marketing.*
>
> *In sales and marketing we had dealers come in and tell us what they wanted in a car to make it more user-friendly, to make it adapt to a customer, based on problems they saw on the floor in selling.*
>
> *"We had insurance companies—Allstate, State Farm, American Road . . . [tell us] how to design a car so when accidents occur it would minimize the customer's expense in fixing it after a collision." One of the problems mentioned by insurance companies was the difficulty in realigning a car that had suffered front-end damage. As a result, Taurus and Sable have cross marks engraved on a suspension tower under the hood to define the center of gravity as an aid in front-end alignment. Team Taurus included Ford's legal and safety advisers, who advised on forthcoming trends in the laws so "we could design for them rather than patching later on" (Walton, 1986, p. 98).*

They also brought manufacturing into the act very early. They went to the stamping and assembly plants and put layouts on the walls. They asked manufacturing how to make it easier to build. They talked to the hourly workers, not just to their supervisors. They collected thousands of suggestions and incorporated most of them. To quote Veraldi again, "It's amazing the dedication and commitment you can get from people. . . . We will never go back to the old ways because we know so much [about] what they can bring to the party."

CHANGE IS NEVER EASY

As with any new approach, there were those in the early stages of the program who were not convinced that this new way was valid. In an early meeting, after Mulally explained the principles to a large group of managers, one of them stood up and asked, "Are you saying I have to remove fear and intimidation from my tool kit?"

Mulally's response was slow, considered, and respectful. "I think so. I don't think we can get there any other way."

The manager was clearly concerned. "I'm not sure I can do that," he said.

"That's okay," said Mulally. "But if you can't, then move on to something else."

* * * * *

THE MAN BEHIND THE PRINCIPLES

In understanding the principles of Boeing's Working Together approach, it is helpful to know something about the man who champions them. Alan Mulally is the charismatic senior vice president of The Boeing Company and president of Commercial Airplanes, a position to which he was named in September 1998. He has held numerous positions since joining Boeing as an engineer in 1969. His bio, which you can read on Boeing's Web site, www.boe-

Alan Mulally

ing.com, reads like a veritable Who's Who. He has received such honors as being elected a Fellow of the American Institute of Aeronautics and Astronautics, was named Engineering Employee of the Year by Boeing in 1978, and was selected by the *Puget Sound Business Journal* as one of the twenty-five business leaders for the 1990s. He holds BS and MS degrees in aeronautical and astronautical engineering from the University of Kansas, and a master's in management from the Massachusetts Institute of Technology, as a 1982 Alfred P. Sloan Fellow. He has been serving on the advisory boards of NASA, the University of Washington, the University of Kansas, the Massachusetts Institute of Technology, and the U.S. Air Force Scientific Advisory Board.

He also serves as a member of the U.S. National Academy of Engineering and England's Royal Academy of Engineering and Royal Aeronautical Society. Alan is a private pilot and really enjoys helping his wife, Nicki, with taxi and cheerleading support for their children, Christopher, Timothy, Amanda, Molly, and Peter.

The proof of the kind of individual and manager he is can be found in the impressions that Boeing employees have of him.

On the day before my first meeting with Mulally in September 2000, I met with Captain John Cashman, the test pilot who flew the first 777. Mulally's secretary, Kay Sigmund, arranged for Boeing transportation to pick me up at my hotel and take me to Cashman's office, so I didn't have to wander around lost in the huge Boeing complex. The driver invited me to get into the front seat with him. He introduced himself as Bruce Jamieson, and we started talking about my meetings with Cashman and Mulally.

"They're both really nice guys," Jamieson told me. "Mr. Mulally is the kind of guy who will pick you out in a big crowd and come over and shake your hand." There was an unspoken suggestion that he might have added, "even when you're just a driver." Certainly in the huge assembly of over 97,000 Boeing employees, a driver may not rank very high in the hierarchy, yet Alan Mulally, president of Boeing Commercial Airplanes, which does some $50 billion in annual sales, would take time to talk to one of their drivers.

During that day and the next I had five different drivers, and every one of them sang the praises of their president. I was convinced, before it was over, that if anyone were to say anything against Alan Mulally in the presence of one of these drivers, that person would have been thoroughly thrashed. Such was their regard for this man. I later learned that this was a sentiment shared by every person I met. When I finally got to meet him the next day, I understood why they were so enthusiastic about Alan Mulally.

When I arrived at the reception area of Alan Mulally's office on Friday, Beth Kerr, his customer relations manager, came down to escort me to his office. She talked with me on the elevator about Alan Mulally and how people in Boeing regard him. She said that there was a strike shortly after he became president, and he lost a lot of sleep because he got personally involved in the situation. Several times he stopped his car at the picket lines and talked with the striking workers—actions that concerned the security people to no end. But this was a man who cared about the workers and wanted to settle this situation as peacefully and fairly as possible.

To make a long story short, I talked with four other people that day and every one of them spoke highly of their president. I have met several company presidents, and many vice presidents, and I have never met one who received such high "marks" from his or her employees. Furthermore, in praising Mulally, not a single person with whom I spoke was at all hesitant in his or her admiration for him. My only concern was that it may be mostly Mulally's personality that was the key to his management success, rather than his principles. That concern disappeared in a later meeting with two Boeing managers, but we'll save that for later.

* * * * *

By the time he became president of Commercial Airplanes, the results of the rigorous test program of the 777 were proof to Mulally that the principles were valid. The plane passed its tests with flying colors and was one of the first planes ever to be accepted by an airline on the first test flight by its own pilots, with hardly any "fixes" being called for. And that confirmation continues as the 777 earns kudos from passengers, airlines, and pilots.

An example is what happened to WA001 just recently. Having accomplished its mission, it could have been retired, but a $120 million airplane is a lot of capital to just cast aside, especially when it is a perfectly serviceable plane with a life expectancy of thirty years or more. So Boeing decided to sell the airplane to a company that could use it for its intended purpose—carrying passengers.

Delivery of that historic plane resulted in one more confirmation of the principles. Sherry Mizuta wrote me the following letter to share their experience. "[So we] . . . went to work to bring WA001 back from a test airplane configuration to revenue passenger airplane configuration for . . . [Cathay Pacific]. Last month [December 2000] we delivered WA001 to Cathay and 30 Boeing employees from the 777 program were selected to go on the delivery flight. The note below was written by one of them. It is further testimony of the pride that still emanates when we reflect on what we can do when we choose to work together to accomplish something really special."

> *Gentlemen, just a quick note on the delivery flight/trip to Hong Kong, on WA001. In one word, INCREDIBLE! Being one of the lucky employees to be chosen for this, I have to say the whole experience was amazing. The very best moment . . . sitting up in*

the cockpit, looking down at the lights from fishing boats off the coast of Japan, and quizzing the Cathay pilots on their opinion of WA001. I asked if there were any problems so far, and the response was a firm no, not even anything minor. They showed me that the engines were within 2 degrees of each other, which, they said, was unheard of on a delivery flight. I asked both pilots what other airplanes they have flown, and they listed multiples, from 737's to 747's to Airbus airplanes. I asked what they thought of the 777, and the pilot, Ian, said "WGA." I asked what does that mean, and he said "World's Greatest Airplane." As you can imagine, I fought the urge to go back out to the passenger cabin and wake up everyone who was sleeping and announce this statement to them. (Really, I wanted to run through the aisles, yelling "WGA," at the top of my lungs!) I wish everyone who has worked on the 777 (and WA001) could have heard him say that, and felt the pride I felt right then. Ian also said, that when he runs into Airbus pilots in airports, and they ask him what he's flying now, he says "WGA," and they know which airplane he's talking about. At that moment, he pointed out an Airbus airplane far below us, heading in the same direction, and with a little boastfulness in his voice, he said we'd be passing over them very soon.

To try to keep this short, the rest of the flight and stay in Hong Kong were great . . . I hope that other employees get to do something similar to this in the future. This type of reward/ positive feedback from our actual Customer cannot be duplicated, or ever forgotten. I appreciate the opportunity to not only go on this trip, but to have worked on WA001, with all the people that made it happen.

Thanks

Rob Sather

Program Management, Commercial Delivery Center (personal correspondence to me from Sherry Mizuta, Director of Administration)

Like the odyssey of WA001 and the people who brought it into being, managing anything large is a journey that can only be successful when everyone who participates does his or her part. To me, the spirit of the people who produced the 777 captures the best of humanity, and, like Alan Mulally, I think these principles are the best of management practice. Furthermore, they are principles that apply equally well as guidelines on how to live life in every way, and so they are universal.

I became convinced in a deceptively simple way. I attended Alan Mulally's weekly Business Plan Review meeting.

2

Meetings, Bloody Meetings

*B*ritish comic actor John Cleese, known best to Americans for his role in *Fawlty Towers*, decided that it should be possible to teach dry subjects in a fun way and thus make them easier to learn. So he made a series of educational videos. One of these was entitled *Meetings, Bloody Meetings*. As anyone knows who has spent any time in an organization, most meetings are a fate worse than death, and Cleese's title conveys that quite well.

So being invited to a meeting is usually not the most exciting thing that can happen to someone—yet that is exactly how I was first exposed to Mulally's principles in action. I have already explained in the Preface how the project came about, so I will not repeat that here. Rather, I will describe how the project was kicked off.

THE PROJECT

My initial plan for learning how the principles operate was to interview a number of Boeing employees—both managers and their reports. So I asked Sherry Mizuta to give me the names of some people in Boeing that I could interview. She sent a list of twenty-four people that I could contact, including Jim Jamieson, executive vice president, Airplane Programs; John Cashman, chief pilot; Scott Carson, CFO; and Ron Ostrowski, vice president and general manager of the 777 program. I sent a blanket email to all of them, asking if I could interview them by phone at a later date. Of course, many of them were too busy to spend time with me, but those who did were—like Mulally—excited about the principles and about sharing them with the world.

One of those individuals was Peter Morton, former vice president of People, Boeing's term for Human Resources, who told me to call him one morning at 6:30 A.M., Seattle time. During the conversation, Morton, who is now retired, told me, "If you really want to see Alan's principles in action, you should attend his Business Plan Review (BPR) meeting." I wondered how a meeting could capture the entire Working Together approach, but Morton seemed to know what he was talking about, so I passed his suggestion on to Sherry and Alan, who agreed.

THE BIG EVENT

Sherry told me to be at the administration building by 7:00 A.M., so that she could get me situated in the meeting room. As I am compulsively early to anything important, I arrived at the front door of the administration building at about 6:45, only to find it locked. Fortunately, the weather was fairly good that morning, so standing outside was comfortable. I watched a number of planes pass overhead, and thought about Boeing's role in my life. Since 1969, when I took my first flight, I have flown about 3 million miles, most of which has been on Boeing planes. I have been completely around the world twice, visited twenty-six countries, and met thousands of interesting people. I remembered a comment

Mulally had made to me in our first meeting. "Maybe our real purpose is bringing people together all over the world," he told me. "It's not just about building airplanes."

As I pondered all this and waited, an immense flock of crows flew over, competing with the noise of the airplanes, trying to find a place to feed. With a lot of squawking and jostling around, they finally settled on an adjacent field. For a moment I thought I had entered the Twilight Zone. It was like a scene from Alfred Hitchcock's movie *The Birds*. I wondered briefly if the birds were an omen.

A couple of minutes after seven, the receptionist arrived and let me into the lobby, and within a few minutes, I was in the St. Helens conference room, where other people were already arriving. Outside the room there were tables with bagels, pastries, coffee, bottled water, and other refreshments. At the front of the room was a large white board that covered most of the wall. Eight circular tables, each with six comfortable chairs, filled the room, and along three walls were seats for visitors.

As people filed in, some took seats at tables and some around the perimeter. There were a number of jovial conversations, a couple of close huddles that clearly were business related, and the rest of us just sat quietly and waited. To the right side of the room near the front was a table at which three women sat with computers. They managed the AV equipment and communications link to remote Boeing facilities.

At 7:30 Alan Mulally appeared and started greeting people. "Glad you're here," he said over and over as he worked his way through the group. He welcomed me and continued through the crowd. At 7:45 a slide appeared on the white board, announcing that this was the Business Plan Review meeting for November 30, 2000, and people took that as their cue to take their seats.

At 8:00 A.M. Mulally removed his jacket, then clipped a lapel microphone onto his shirt and kicked off the meeting. He welcomed everyone and moved immediately to a slide that contained the agenda. Then the leadership team was introduced to the visitors, with the injunction to everyone to network with their new teammates. "That's part of what Working Together is all about," Mulally explained. As the leaders were introduced, each of them in turn presented their invited guests, so that everyone was included in the introductions. Sherry Mizuta was introduced, and in turn told the group about me. Alan added that I was writing a book about their principles, "So be nice to him," he said, and everyone laughed.

Some of the leadership team was located at Boeing facilities in Witchita, Kansas; Long Beach, California; and Washington, D.C. They participated over a telecommunications link, introduced their own guests, and so the process continued for about twenty minutes. At that point, Mulally reiterated that he hoped the introductions would be used by everyone present to network with each other.

As I mentioned above, this step demonstrated one of the principles—everyone is included. Members of the team were from every function in the company—manufacturing, engineering, sales, marketing, customer relations, the human resources department (which they call simply "people"). They were all there. Later I realized that because of this, they all understood exactly how they stood in relationship to everyone else, and how the status of another group might affect their own unit, so that they could, if necessary, get together with the other group to coordinate a solution. The efficiency of this process alone must save Boeing a ton of money, not to mention the real benefit, which is to make people feel that they are really a part of everything that is going on so that they can take ownership for solving whatever problems there are.

REVIEW OF THE PRINCIPLES AND THE BUSINESS PLAN

Next Mulally turned to a slide labeled Working Together, which contained the eleven principles that he considers the key to how the business should be managed. He ran through them quickly, with little comment. Once these had been covered, he moved on to his own part of the business data. When he finished, other members of the leadership team took the floor and began covering their own status reports. If there was no change in status from the previous week to the present, they said so and moved on to their next slide. If there was a change, it was announced and discussed briefly. Anything that needed it was assigned to a special attention meeting for follow-up.

Status was shown using graphs in some cases and numerical tables in others, but most commonly there was a system using a "stoplight" metaphor in which boxes are colored red, yellow, or green to show status quickly. A green box signified that everything was okay for that item. Yellow indicated cause for concern, as there was a deviation from plan that exceeded acceptable tolerances. Red, of course, meant that there was a definite problem for that item. If an item had changed from okay to concern, the box would be split in half, with green on the left side and yellow on the right. Conversely, an item that had gotten back on track was shown with yellow on the left side and green on the right.

Mulally and fellow leadership team members asked questions frequently, and these were answered and the process continued quickly. By shortly after nine, he called a break for seven minutes, and people began milling around talking with each other and getting refreshments from the tables outside. At the end of the break they continued with the review. By 10:15, the review was complete. Data for the entire $50 billion operation had been covered with a precision that was a marvel to watch.

But the meeting was not finished. Mulally asked the leadership team members for their thoughts about any other aspects of the plan that needed special attention before the next meeting. Sherry noted their comments and included these special attention items in the plan. He then asked invited guests for their comments, reactions, or whatever they wished to say. One fellow announced that he was a low-ranking employee, and that he was very impressed with what he had seen, and said that he felt even more secure in his job than ever before. Other people voiced similar sentiments.

One person said that he was very impressed with the progress that the leadership team had made since he had been a guest about a year before. Sherry asked for my impression. I said that I was impressed at the organization of the process, the use of technology to tie everyone together, and, most importantly, that I was very impressed to see that they didn't try to solve any problems that were identified during the meeting, which is how so many meetings like this get bogged down.

Several guests noted the camaraderie evidenced by everyone in the room. It really was as if they were one big family, which is not that common for a senior management group.

Mulally ended by saying, "We all now know where we are and what needs to be done and we can go forward, helping each other with confidence that we are all working on the right things. We can also look forward to our progress next week. We know what to do. We don't need to wait for direction. We will not let each other down."

I didn't say so, but many of the project reviews that I have attended have been blood-letting events. People with problems were thoroughly chastised in front of the entire group. In fact, someone commented on this, and Alan said, "If you beat them up for showing red on their progress report, they'll just change it to green next time, even though the problem won't really have been solved." He's right. When I worked at ITT, the culture was management through intimidation. Most people would hide problems until they became impossible to hide, rather than announce a problem and get beaten up for it. I am sure this resulted in problems becoming crises that could have been solved easily if people had felt free to discuss them openly. As one of the Boeing principles says, "We can't manage a secret." Get problems out into the open so that they can be handled.

THE ESSENCE OF MANAGEMENT

In the video on meetings that I mentioned earlier, Cleese makes a tremendously significant point. "The essence of management," he says, "is in how meetings are run." The first time I heard that, I thought, "He is absolutely right." Then it occurred to me that this should scare the daylights out of anyone who has concerns about how organizations are managed, because statistics say that the large majority of meetings are ineffective, time-wasting, costly events that could better be done without. Now, as painful as it

The "essence of management" is in how meetings are run.

may be to admit, if you can't run an effective meeting, how can you expect to run a successful organization?

Interestingly, the things that plague some organizations are seen in meetings. Many meetings (and organizations) have no clear objective or mission, and even when there is a stated objective, people often don't stick to it. The meeting loses focus. People get bogged down trying to solve whatever problems are reported and this drags on until half the people present wish they could substitute a horse-whipping for having to stay in the meeting. Finally everyone crawls out, weary of the entire proceeding and hoping they can get out of the next such corporate hell.

This meeting was *very* different. It had a clear objective. The agenda spelled out exactly what was to be accomplished, and everyone stuck to task. There were no side conversations, no fights, and no groans from the audience. They started on time and ended on time. There was a lot of camaraderie, people enjoying each other, celebrating achievements that had happened during the last week, and assurances that various problems were being addressed, with specific actions being outlined.

You could not watch this process without having a warm fuzzy feeling about how the company as a whole was being managed. It is hard to believe that such organization could exist in the meeting and that chaos could exist in the day-to-day operation itself. I considered applying for a job myself, because I have always dreamed of working for an organization that is really well managed, and I felt that I had found one at last!

A FACE-TO-FACE INTERVIEW

After the meeting, I met with Rick Gardner, who is in Program Management for Airplane Programs, and Marty Bentroitt, who is in Sales. We talked about the meeting and about the principles and their experience with them. Both enthusiastically endorsed the principles. Rick had worked at Boeing ever since graduating from college, so he had no experience at other companies, but he had experience in Boeing before Mulally started applying the principles and was quick to say that things were much better now. He agreed that most reporting in the old days was an attempt to cover your behind when you were having problems and to dodge bullets.

The question is, I said, whether these principles can be rolled out into other organizations and make them work. It is clear to anyone who has ever met Alan Mulally that the man is in some part responsible for the success of the principles just by force of his personality. He is charismatic. He is friendly, genuinely caring about people, and he always puts a positive spin on even the worst disaster—simply asking everyone to sit down together and find a way to deal with the problem. If he is ever depressed or taken down by a situation, he never shows it, they told me.

But to answer my question, Rick said that he had about 100 people in his group, and he added, "I'm not very charismatic. Neither is [another manager whom I know]. But all we have to do is explain the principles to our people and 'walk the talk' and they get it." Marty said the same thing. He was certain that the principles would transfer anywhere—as long as one condition exists. That is, the president, CEO, or whatever the title of the top manager, must wholeheartedly believe in the principles and persist in applying them in spite of adversity.

The principles do not form a program of the month. They are not a gimmick. They are an integrated philosophy of how a company conducts itself in the world in relation to its customers, suppliers, employees, and the communities in which they live. That is why these principles are so powerful, and that is why they will help a company succeed and survive in the most turbulent of times. I am convinced of that.

They reflect character—moral, ethical, and social conscience—and in terms of the struggle between good and evil, these principles are on the side of good and must prevail in the long run. The principle-centered organization has a competitive advantage over those companies that have no principles.

Furthermore, the effect that these principles have on the employees at Boeing, together with their customers and key suppliers, brings out the best and most noble that is possible for human beings to express. The principles promote self-actualization. They encourage fair and equitable treatment of people. And they support everyone having a good time doing what most people would call work, but under such conditions, *work* may not be the most appropriate word. Indeed, this kind of work is more like play, and who would not want to spend their lives playing, if given the choice?

If I sound zealous about the philosophy, I am. If I seem dogmatic about the principles, I freely admit it. I have spent nearly forty years wading through the swamp of management literature, a lot of it written by people who have never managed, and I can tell you that I wish that long ago I had worked in a company managed by these principles. I could have thrown away most of those tomes, and it would have saved me from reading a lot of nonsense.

Applying these principles in your teams or organizations promises to be an exciting adventure. As one of the principles says: Enjoy the journey!

3

Working Together

There is only one reason for having more than one person in an enterprise—he or she can't do everything that needs to be done to meet the needs of the customer. Henry Ford built his first automobile entirely by himself in a small shed behind his house. But he couldn't build very many cars that way, so he had to start hiring people to meet the demand. Furthermore, he couldn't make every single part of the car, so he had to start buying those parts from other suppliers. Most organizations are forced to go in this direction eventually, although some, like General Motors, try to decrease their dependence on suppliers by buying them, but this sometimes backfires. However, even if they were to make every single part that goes into their products, companies still have to obtain their raw materials from vendors, so they always have some dependence on the external environment for their inputs.

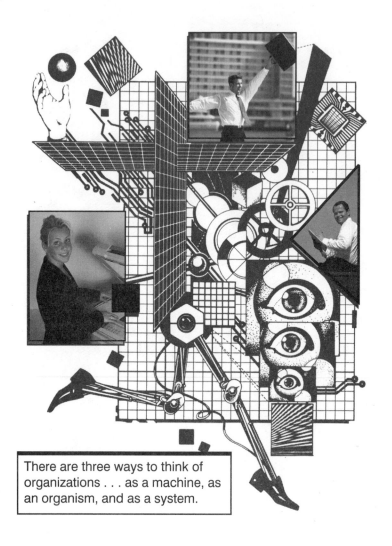

There are three ways to think of organizations . . . as a machine, as an organism, and as a system.

CONCEPTS OF ORGANIZATIONS

Once you have more than one person doing various jobs to achieve a final result, you have an organization. There are three ways to think of organizations: as a machine, as an organism, or as a system. The earliest concept was the machine model, because of the influence of physics. Science at that time tried to understand the universe and everything in it using machine concepts. To understand a machine, you break it down into its parts and analyze them. The aggregate behavior of those parts explains the behavior of the machine itself.

The organismic view treats an organization as a living thing. Notice that *organization* and *organism* have the same root. A machine has no inherent purpose. It is an inanimate thing that functions only the way a living entity makes it function. An organism, however, does have a purpose. At the very least, that purpose is survival, and usually to reproduce itself for the survival of the species itself. Thinking of organizations as organisms leads to the concept that the organization needs to survive and thrive.

Finally, an organization can be thought of as a system. This is the contemporary view. A system also has a purpose, but cannot be understood by analysis of its individual parts. Furthermore, there are two kinds of systems: those that are closed to the outside environment and are therefore not affected by it and those that are open to influence from outside. Organizations are clearly open systems. In fact, they are *social* systems, being comprised of people.

The following premises are useful in thinking of organizations as systems. A *system* is a whole that contains two or more parts that satisfy the following five conditions:

1. The whole has one or more defining functions. As an example, an automobile's defining function is to transport people on land. The defining function of a brewer is to make and sell beer.

2. Each part in the set can affect the behavior or properties of the whole. For example, the heart, lungs, and stomach can affect the properties of the entire body (although the body is an organism, it is also a system). The engine in a car can affect the performance of the whole, although the glove compartment cannot. The glove compartment is like the appendix in the body—an add-on that is not known to have a function so far as the entire system is concerned.

3. There is a subset of parts that is sufficient for carrying out the defining function of the whole. Each part is necessary but insufficient for carrying out this defining

The parts of a system interact.

function. The automobile engine, wheels, battery, and steering wheel are essential. However, the radio, ashtray, and clock are not essential for transporting people, but they enhance the function of the car.

3. The way that the behavior or properties of each part of a system affects its behavior depends on the behavior or properties of at least one other part of the system. In other words, no part of a system has an independent effect on the system. The parts of a system *interact,* either directly or indirectly. Again, as an example, the effect of the lungs on the body depends on what the heart, brain, and other parts are doing.

4. The effect of any subset of parts on the system as a whole depends on the behavior of at least one other subset. Like the individual parts of the system, the subsets also interact. The effect of the metabolic subsystem depends on the behavior of the nervous subsystem (Ackoff, 1994, pp. 18–21).

THE NEED TO WORK TOGETHER

Once you understand that an organization is a social system and that its overall performance depends on the *interactions* among its parts and its *environment*—rather than being determined by the specific actions of the parts themselves—you can quickly see why the way in which organizations interact with their suppliers and customers becomes important. The internal interactions are equally important. The accounting and engineering departments cannot independently design, produce, and deliver an airplane or any other product. Neither can the manufacturing department. As one of the systems concepts states, No single part of the system can perform the defining function of the entire system. The engine of a car cannot move people by itself. All of the parts must *work together* to achieve the desired result—this is a law! Furthermore, since an open system interacts with its environment, which includes customers and suppliers, this means there must be *coordinated, cooperative* effort if an organization is to thrive and survive in an increasingly global, competitive business environment.

Interestingly, for many years we believed that the engineering department could design a product all by itself—totally independently of customers or the people who had to make the product. And this belief led to products that were disasters, because the market didn't accept them.

> *All significant multidisciplinary efforts require coordinated, cooperative effort—commonly called teamwork.*

Strangely, despite many examples that show the need to involve all stakeholders in developing a product or service, we still see companies developing things in disregard of customers, suppliers, and other parties affected by them. Further, we see a throw-it-over-the-wall approach in many companies that engage in product development. The cost is enormous. All significant multidisciplinary efforts require coordinated, cooperative effort—commonly called teamwork. But how do you achieve it?

COOPERATIVE EFFORT

We Americans have a love-hate relationship with teamwork. On the one hand, we have numerous sports teams, in which every

WORKING TOGETHER is the grand principle of management.

player knows that cooperation is necessary to win a game. On the other hand, even in those teams there is always tension between cooperation and competition. The superstar player gets a lot of attention and may be tempted to think that he or she *is* the team. Too much of that attitude, however, and the other players get resentful and quit feeding that player the ball, and he or she quickly finds that no one can be a superstar without the supporting actions of teammates.

The superstar can't win the game alone!

I believe it is important to realize that programs involving thousands of people are too complex to be thought of as teams, but they certainly require cooperative effort. So the Working Together principles are not just a special case of principles for managing teams, nor do they advocate that an organization must be team-based. They simply recognize the need for coordinated, cooperative effort and also the need for certain ways of behaving in the context of the workplace.

True partnering occurs when customers and suppliers participate directly and regularly in the decision-making process.

WORKING WITH THE CUSTOMER

Prior to the development of the 777, Boeing also designed airplanes using a throw-it-over-the-wall approach. But with the 777, the stakes were very high, and Boeing needed an airline to commit to buy a certain number of them, or their huge investment would be at great risk. Sabbagh (1996) has documented the intensive round-the-clock negotiations that took place between Boeing and United Airlines, so I will only summarize the final outcome.

Essentially United had to decide between Boeing and Airbus, and since the decision involved billions of dollars Jim Guyette, executive vice president at United, was on the firing line. If he made the wrong decision, his name would be mud. He was leaning toward recommending that United go with Boeing and the 777, but what if he was wrong? The intense pressure apparently caused him to wake up in a cold sweat during the middle of the night, around 2:15 A.M. He got up and wrote a memo on a hotel notepad, one of those little pads they leave by the phone in every sleeping room. It said:

> We agree to work together to deliver a service-ready airplane, an airplane that works.

"And then he dragged Phil Condit and Dick Albrecht (a senior Boeing sales executive) into the room, and he said, 'Will you sign this?' And he took that to Mr. Wolf, and he said, 'This is the new Boeing. The new Boeing is going to treat us at a new level of respect as a customer and for the next five years they are going to work with us to deliver something Boeing's never delivered before on any other airplane'" (Sabbagh, 1996, p. 53).

In making this agreement, United and Boeing agreed to work together to produce a new airplane that would not just be designed by Boeing—it would be *jointly* designed! This became the theme of the 777 development program. *Working together,* we will design and build the world's best airplane, they proclaimed.

A MAJOR CHANGE

This change to a cooperative venture was more profound than it may seem. Not only did companies design products in isolation from their customers, but the throw-it-over-the-wall method of doing things means that they didn't even cooperate *internally!* Perhaps I should say that many *still* don't cooperate internally. At the simplest level, we find that people won't share information with each other, much less cooperate in other ways. Managers, especially, withhold information from people who report to them, because they have learned that privileged information gives them power. But lacking certain information, their direct reports can't make good decisions or take appropriate steps to solve problems.

We also find that many employees compete with each other, rather than cooperating, because they view the world in dog-eat-dog terms. It is based on the scarcity principle that dominates economic thinking. At the personal level, the view is that if each individual doesn't grab her piece of the pie, the other "dogs" will get it, and she will wind up empty-handed. Unfortunately, there is some truth in this, so the belief is confirmed, and it is very hard to convince people that they could be more successful through internal cooperation than through competition. Their competition should be directed at the other organization, not other members of their own company.

I have sometimes been surprised at how strong this tendency is, and one example stands out in my mind. In the early design of my seminar on how to plan, schedule, and control projects, I developed a scheduling exercise in which a group of bank robbers was planning a robbery. They planned to pick the lock on the back door of a bank, and they would then enter the bank, clean out the cash drawers and safe, then exit through that same door. They knew that an alarm would sound at the police station in the process, and they knew how long it would take the police to reach the bank, so they were trying to sequence all of the steps to see if they could pull off the robbery before the police arrived.

The crucial question was whether the alarm would sound when they picked the lock or when they actually pulled open the door. In the seminar, the participants split up into arbitrary groups, and each group was trying to solve the scheduling problem. Since the data sheet that I gave them did not specify when the alarm would sound, they usually asked me about it. In most instances, I would tell them to try it both ways.

However, in one public seminar, a fellow came to me and asked when the alarm went off, and I said, "Why don't you ask the expert?" He asked who that might be.

"That lady over there is a bank vice president," I said. "If anyone would know, she probably would."

It was his response that floored me. "Oh, can we ask her?" he said. "She's not in our group."

That one comment spoke volumes about the problems we have with this principle. She's not in our group, so we can't ask her for help.

Can we ask her? She's not on our team!

I wanted to ask, "Who told you that you were competing with each other? I certainly didn't."

This was not, of course, an isolated incident. I experienced it early in my career, when I proposed to a class that an organization can only be successful if the members keep internal competition to a minimum and compete only with other companies. A woman in my class got extremely indignant and angrily told me that this was ridiculous. "Everyone is competitive," she declared, adding that my suggestion was silly and out of touch with reality. I tried to explain that competition and cooperation are opposite ends of a stick, and that when people compete they can't achieve goals that require collective effort. She was not swayed by my explanation. She was convinced that competition was the only way to survive in this world, and, by golly, any suggestion to the contrary was ludicrous.

Of course, not every individual is totally competitive by nature, but those who want to be cooperative often find their behavior resisted or taken advantage of by the competitive people with whom they deal. Extensive research on cooperation versus competition has shown that, when one person or group in an interaction adopts a competitive stance, the other party soon abandons cooperation and becomes competitive (Axelrod, 1984).

We see this "looking out for number one" as self-interest. The "golden rule" is modified to "do unto others before they can do unto you." But consultant Peter Block (2000) has written that enlightened self-interest would best be achieved by realizing that one's personal objectives are best met through cooperation and doing what is best for the overall organization than through competition or totally self-serving actions.

To understand this, remember that a system is a thing in which individual parts can affect the functioning of the whole. If you do something to damage the functioning of one part of a system, you are almost certain to affect the overall system performance. As an example, if the lungs are not functioning properly, there will not be enough oxygen getting to other systems and not enough waste being removed from them, so that they will begin to deteriorate, and if this process is not checked, the entire organism will die.

> *If any individual member of an organization does something that hurts one part of the enterprise, that effect will harm the entire system.*

Therefore, if any individual member of an organization does something that hurts one part of the enterprise, that effect will harm the entire system sooner or later. So if we were to install a procedure in the engineering department that somehow degraded the performance of that department, that effect will be felt in the entire system.

REWARD SYSTEMS

If you want cooperation, you must reward cooperation, not competition, which is exactly what some companies do. You cannot reward competition and expect to get cooperation! For organizations that make use of a lot of teams, part of a person's rewards must come from contributions to the team and part from individual performance.

> *You must reward what you want, not what you don't want!*

However, our belief in the value of competition is so strong that I have known companies to set up internal competitions between teams in an attempt to boost productivity, only to have such programs blow up on them. This happened in a textile mill. They created a shift-to-shift competition. They had a round-the-clock, three-shift operation, and they declared that the team (treating each shift as a big team) that had the highest production for the week would be eligible for a prize. The prize was for every member of the team—together with their significant others—to receive a dinner at a prestigious steak house in the area.

Apparently this was a desirable award, because things started humming. However, the employees weren't content to just produce more. People on one team soon realized that if they were to misadjust the machines at the end of their shift so that they wouldn't run well for the team that followed, this would cost the next team precious time resetting the machines, and give the first team an advantage. Naturally it took only a day or two for the abused team to realize what was being done to them, so they did the same thing to the team following them, and this was repeated, so that it became a contest for each team to see just how much they could screw up a machine to slow down the next group.

> *Competition often becomes destructive.*

When management found out what was happening, they had to make a new rule: To be eligible for the award, the team that followed would have to report that every machine ran well when they came on duty.

This episode demonstrates what can happen when people inside a company begin competing with other members of the same company—that competition often turns into "dirty tricks." In other words, it becomes *destructive,* rather than constructive.

IMPROVING EMPLOYEE PERFORMANCE

As I explained above, an organization conceived as a machine has no purpose of its own, but exists solely to serve the purposes of its owners, and that usually means making a profit. An organization seen as a social system, however, is an entirely different matter. Not only does the enterprise have a purpose but so do the constituent parts. It is not too hard to see this when you consider the term *empire building.* Managers of departments are sometimes guilty of trying to build their own little empires within an overall enterprise because they feel more powerful when they have bigger departments, get more rewards, or whatever. However, as we have seen, such empire building is not necessarily in the interest of overall organizational performance. In fact, it may do definite harm to the enterprise.

What is important to understand is that every employee in the company has his or her own ideals, interests, and purposes, and in the view of an organization as a machine, these were ignored. People were viewed as replaceable parts. As managers began to realize that an enterprise is a social system, however, they also realized that they could not ignore the concerns of their employees.

> *Every employee in the company has his or her own ideals, interests, and purposes.*

Furthermore, they began to ask themselves how to get the best performance from those expensive, often hard-to-replace employees. Perhaps if they were paid more. Or maybe they would work harder if they were given titles. Then again, perhaps training them was the answer. These are questions of motivation and skill development. And, while it seems obvious that motivating an unskilled employee won't necessarily improve his performance, we have seen this approach

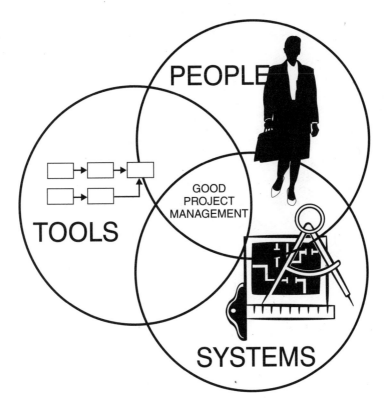

Figure 3.1
Tools, people, systems.

tried. We have also seen the opposite—give employees skills without giving them the motivation to use those skills. Any way you think about it, improving the performance of people is a central concern of every organization.

There are three components of an organization that must be dealt with to get good results. Good performance occurs at the intersection of tools, people, and systems. This means that giving people greater skills alone won't necessarily improve organizational results. Nor will motivating them. Remember, the parts interact. See Figure 3.1.

Quality circles were the big rage in the early 1980s, but many failed because we gave the team members training in technical things like problem-solving, Pareto analysis, and presentation skills without giving them skills in how to work together. We took for granted that people know how to work in teams, when that simply

People often have to be taught how to work in teams.

is not true in many cases. Because American society has for so long been oriented to individual performance, people do not always know how to cooperate and collaborate, and this must be taught.

QUALITY OF WORK LIFE

Motivation has been defined as the drive one has to satisfy his or her needs. As most people know, Abraham Maslow studied human needs and decided that all of them can be placed into five categories. These are *physiological, security or safety, social, self-esteem,* and *self-actualization.* The term *self-actualization* means the individual's drive to be everything he or she is capable of being. It is full expression of oneself.

Motivation is the drive to satisfy needs.

Maslow hypothesized that these categories are organized as a hierarchy, with physiological needs at the bottom and self-actualization at the top as shown in Figure 3.2. He proposed that as lowerlevel needs are met, higher-level needs become more important. Research has never

Figure 3.2
Maslow's hierarchy.

been able to conclusively validate that the order is as postulated by Maslow, so we will forget about that point for this discussion. We do know that "To the extent that organizations are designed to meet lower-level needs exclusively, high performance is unlikely to occur" (Pasmore, 1988, p. 28). The reason for this will become clear later on.

We also know that when the two lower-level needs are met (the need for food, clothing, shelter, and health), the individual becomes more concerned with the quality of life. *Quality of life* is defined as the satisfaction (or fun) we get from doing what we do regardless of what we do it for and a sense of progress toward becoming more competent to meet our needs over time. "The higher our standard of living, the more consideration we give to the fun we derive from what we do and its *meaningfulness*" (Ackoff, 1994, p. 71, emphasis added). The quality-of-life issue affects us both on and off the job.

In the view of an organization as mechanistic or organic, work was not supposed to be fun, fulfilling, or meaningful. These properties have relevance only if people are treated as purposeful, not as organs or parts of a machine. The systems view of the enterprise recognizes that this view is invalid. People have purpose, and they expect to have those purposes met in the conduct of their jobs.

As Peter Drucker has argued, "Employees have to be managed as partners. The management of people is a marketing job. In marketing, one does not begin with the question, 'What do WE want?' One begins with the question: 'What does the other party want?'" (Drucker, 1999, p. 21). We know that highest organization performance is achieved when workers are enabled to meet their personal needs in performing to meet the organization's needs. And quality of life at work is one of those personal needs or if not a need, at least an expectation.

In fact, this is a big failing for many organizations. Viktor Frankl has proposed that a commanding drive for human beings is to find meaning in life. He contends that a crucial cause of personal and, consequently, social ills is that people find life to be meaningless (Frankl, 1984). Recently, Michael Lerner wrote a book entitled *The Politics of Meaning*, in which he reports studies in workplaces that tried to determine what people find rewarding in their jobs and also what they wanted from those jobs. The researchers believed when they started their studies that they would find workers complaining about low pay and benefits. Instead they found people saying that their jobs were mindless and meaningless. People felt that their jobs should more properly be done by robots rather than by human beings (Lerner, 1996).

Other studies have found that job simplification, while it allows people to learn their jobs and become productive quickly, ultimately leads to the feeling of boredom, frustration, and burnout. People do not thrive on simplification, but on a certain level of complexity. This finding has led to techniques commonly called *job enlargement* and *job enrichment*, and are exemplified by such devices as self-directed work teams (Lawler, etc.).

Ackoff offers a simple test for determining the extent to which a job meets the conditions for quality-of-work life. Simply ask a person, "Suppose you are told right now that you will continue to draw your current salary in constant dollars for the rest of your life and you need not work anymore to receive it. What would you do tomorrow?" If the answer is anything but "I would come back to work tomorrow and do exactly what I am doing today," the quality-of-work life needs improvement (Ackoff, 1994, p. 74.).

He goes on to say that, "The higher the quality of work life the producers of products or services enjoy, the higher the quality of products or services they produce. . . . Those who do not enjoy a high quality of work life transform their dissatisfaction with their work into the poor quality of products and services they produce. The current plethora of programs to increase quality of outputs cannot succeed unless the quality of the input, the work life that went into them is also high" (op cit., p. 74).

> *The higher the quality-of-work life for employees, the higher their performance will be.*

The question is, how can an organization improve the quality-of-work life for its members? In the first place, it is virtually impossible to measure or assess whether quality-of-work life is high or low, much less improve it as managers. "However," says Ackoff, "if those whose quality of life is involved were given an opportunity to affect that quality significantly, there would be no need for others to try to do it for them. *People who can make quality-of-life decisions for themselves have less of an evaluative problem than others who try to make these decisions for them.* Once planners and managers give up the idea of redesigning the work of others and, instead, give them an opportunity to design their own work and work environment, they have no difficulty in bringing about changes that lead to significant improvements in their quality of work life" (Ackoff, 1994, p. 77).

What Ackoff is saying means that organizations cannot continue to be organized and managed as if they are mechanical or organic structures. We must recognize that they are social systems, in which the members have purposes of their own, and that these members must be allowed to participate in decisions that concern them, so that they experience a higher quality-of-work life. Hence, when this is done, we can expect that their productivity and quality

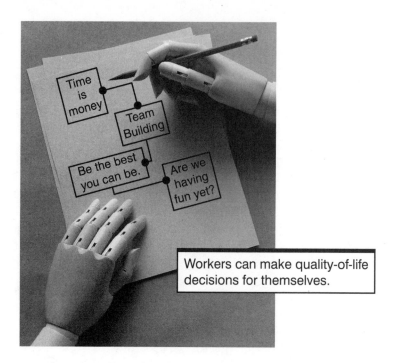

of work will increase. Since this is the ultimate concern of most managers, it seems reasonable to say that the Working Together Principles and Practices that follow must be the guiding principles of organizations that want to survive and thrive in this turbulent, global economy that we now live in. The remainder of this book will focus on the principles that must be part of a Working Together approach to managing an organization.

4

You Must Have a Compelling Vision

On several occasions I have stood on the Salisbury Plains in England and wondered at the marvel that is called Stonehenge. The stones are immense and are known to have been hauled about 13 miles over the plains from the quarry. The structure was apparently built in three stages between 3000 and 1000 B.C. This in itself raises tremendous questions.

Did a continuous line of people maintain a culture for 2000 years? Did they pass down the function of Stonehenge? Were they improving it as they learned more about the movement of the stars and planets?

Why the structure was built remains a mystery, but the evidence is compelling for an astronomical explanation. It seems to be, essentially, a huge calendar of sorts, marking the equinoxes.

Photo by Jim Lewis

This must have been important to the people who put an enormous amount of hours of exhausting labor into its construction.

A manager must get people to perform above the minimum acceptable level.

I began wondering about motivation as a young engineering manager about thirty-five years ago, and studied the subject intensively when I later earned my doctorate in psychology. The big question for organizations always has been how to get people to perform beyond minimal acceptable levels. Think about that. Minimal acceptable performance is survival level. No organization wants to simply survive. They want to grow and develop themselves, as I discussed in Chapter 3.

So as you read about and visit the megaliths that people have built around the world, you can't help but ask the question, "How did the leaders of these people get them to put in the effort required over the large time spans involved?" Truly this represents leadership and motivation at its best.

Certainly some of this work may have been done by slave labor, but there is evidence that much of it was done by the people themselves, and not under tyrannical leaders. When tyranny persists for very long, people tend to rebel and overthrow the tyrants, so I don't think the projects can be dismissed so easily as the efforts of slaves.

DOING SOMETHING MEANINGFUL

Remember Viktor Frankl's contention that a core concern of people is to find meaning in life? I believe that these projects were viewed by the people who did the actual manual labor as incredi-

Nothing happens unless
first a dream
— Carl Sandburg

bly important. In the case of the people who built Stonehenge and the Mayas, there is evidence that they were very concerned with the calendar, with predicting when the seasons would begin and end. For the Mayas, experts have suggested that this may have meant the difference between death and survival. The reason is that knowing when to plant crops was very important, just as it is to farmers today. The Mayas had no farmer's almanacs to guide them (nor any printed calendars for that matter) so they tried to develop ways of measuring time through physical structures. The Mayas built quite a few structures that seem to have served the function of measuring time through observation of the heavens.

What I am suggesting is that these people were motivated by the belief that what they were doing was tremendously important. They had a *vision* of what the outcome of their efforts would do for them, and this is a key that you will find in almost every past or present example of significant human accomplishment.

As Ackoff has written, "A sense of progress toward ideals gives life meaning, makes choice significant. However, today many feel that they have little real choice, no control over their futures. They are driven to fatalism, resignation to a future that they believe is determined by the past rather than by what they do" (Ackoff, 1994, p. 75). If you consider the effect of such mind-sets on organizations, you can see that many of today's workers (at all levels, not just blue-collar) are alienated, jaded, and find themselves in a rut. Studies have found that nearly 85 percent of executives report not being happy with their work lives. If this is true of executives, how can people at lower levels in the hierarchy possibly fare any better?

BEYOND MOTIVATION: AROUSING PASSION IN PEOPLE

I believe that what really drove the builders of the world's great monuments was *passion*—a tremendous drive to do something great. And, if that is true, then the leader's job is to arouse in people a passion for what they are doing. Roz and Ben Zander say that, "Life flows when we put our attention on the larger patterns of which we are a part . . . life takes on shape and meaning when a person is able to transcend the barriers of personal survival and become a unique conduit for its vital energy" (Zander and Zander, 2000, p. 117). They are discussing their practice of giving way to passion. "The access to passion gives momentum to efforts to build a business plan, it gives a reason to set up working teams, it gives power to settling individual demands, and it gives urgency to communicating across sections of a company" (op cit., p. 119).

We must go beyond motivation—we must arouse passion in people!

While I was writing another chapter, I got a phone call from Ron Ostrowski, vice president and general manager of the 777 program at Boeing. It was January 3, and Ron said he had just

PRINCIPLE: You must have a compelling vision.

read an article in the *Seattle Times* about the Huskies, who had just won the Rose Bowl. Their coach, Rick Neuheisel, was interviewed and he talked about the need to arouse the *emotion* of players, to get them really charged up about a game, if they were going to perform well. "It's not about the trophy," Neuheisel said. "It's about the climb to the trophy" (*Seattle Times*, January 3, 2001). He said that the emotion all of them felt in playing—and winning—was what was really important, and that they would never forget that feeling, and people who had not been a part of it would never know that feeling.

This article caused Ron to start thinking about the Boeing principles, and he decided to call to share his thoughts with me. "We talk a lot about the principles," he said, "but we don't talk much about arousing emotion in people." I agreed with him. I told him about a time years ago when I got a bit upset about something at work, and my boss told me that I should leave my emotions outside when I came to work. Yet in the next breath, he wanted me to be motivated to do my job. What he overlooked is that *emotion* and *motivated* have a common root, Old French *emouvoir*, "stir up," and Latin *emovere*, "move out" (Barnhart, 1995).

What my boss was really saying was that he wanted me to leave any *negative* emotions I might have outside, but to bring into the workplace my *positive* emotions! Well, it's a nice sentiment, but it doesn't work. People bring with them into the workplace the good, the bad, the ugly, and it is a manager's job to harness the good and minimize expression of the bad and ugly. In fact, I believe that the more successful we are in arousing the passion of people, the less we will see the negative aspects of their behavior.

> *People bring with them into the workplace the good, the bad, the ugly, and it is a manager's job to harness the good.*

If we return to Maslow's need hierarchy, presented in Chapter 3, it seems clear that there is a vast qualitative difference in the kind of motivation people feel for the lower levels of the pyramid (see Figure 4.1). The lower levels provide motivation all right. If I am hungry or cold I want to relieve the discomfort I feel. I may even get a little desperate the more intense the hunger and cold become. But desperation is not the same thing as passion.

It is when I move up to the higher levels that I find people getting passionate about something. Maslow talked about self-actualization being the pinnacle of the hierarchy, but I think he may have overlooked something. *Self-actualization* is a term he coined to mean that we have a drive to be everything we are capable of being. Now I don't know if he meant for this to include the pursuit of ideas and dreams, but it seems clear to me that these are the true drivers for people. Dreams, ideas, and visions give people a sense of purpose, which, as mentioned in Chapter 3, is of major concern for every individual.

As Kevin and Jackie Freiberg say in their book about Southwest Airlines, "There are no heights to which the human spirit can't rise when people see that their work has meaning and purpose. People *want* to make a difference. . . . When we know that our work is meaningful, we still have energy at the end of the day because the sanctity of our labor has been affirmed. The people at Southwest Airlines don't work there just because the company is thriving; they work there because they see how the company's

Figure 4.1
Maslow's hierarchy.

fight to survive is tied up in their own need to make a difference in society" (Freiberg and Freiberg, 1996, p. 321).[1]

PASSION IS INSATIABLE

I believe the most important thing to understand about motivation is that the lower-level needs represent things that can be fairly easily met and that, once met, no longer drive a person. The higher needs, on the other hand, such as recognition, self-esteem, and purpose are virtually insatiable. A person almost never gets

---

1. I am indebted to Ron Ostrowski for suggesting this book to me during our conversation.

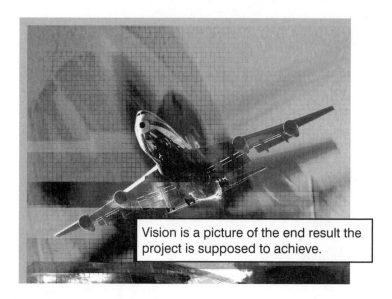

Vision is a picture of the end result the
project is supposed to achieve.

enough of these. And these needs are what managers must arouse
if they are going to get *greatness* from people!

WHAT IS VISION?

What is a compelling vision? In fact, what is vision itself? I have
found that people are confused by the difference between mission
and vision. That is easy to understand when you find the terms
being used in different ways in management literature. So I am
going to offer a definition. Whether it agrees with those of others
is not very important as long as you understand what I am con-
veying.

Vision is a picture of the end result that the project is supposed
to achieve. It's that simple. However, it is not so easy to achieve a
shared vision throughout the project team, and yet this is necessary
if that vision is to be achieved.

The mission of the project team is to achieve the vision. The vision for the 777 program was that it would be intermediate in size
between the 747 and 767, a plane that would be the most technologically advanced in the world, and one that would take them
into the twenty-first century well positioned in the marketplace.
Mulally simplified that vision by drawing a little cartoon that said,
"Denver to Honolulu on a hot day." This is shown in Figure 4.2.

Figure 4.2
Mulally's button.

This cartoon was soon made into a button that people wore—thereby keeping the vision ever present in the minds of everyone working on the program.

The mission, then, was to achieve the vision—that is, to develop an airplane that would meet those requirements. Here is the point. It is not enough to say, "Our mission is to develop a 777 airplane," and just stop there. People have to know what kind of airplane the 777 will be. Is it like a 737? How big is it? How many engines

> *A dream need not be immense in scale, but it must be large enough to house a multitude.*
> —Warren Bennis

does it have? What must be its range? All of these questions can be answered by the specifications, but specs are cold and uninspiring. The vision for the 777 went beyond the specifications. It will be technologically superior to anything else available to the airplanes. It will be such a good airplane that the pilots will love

47

it, the passengers will love it, and the airlines will flock to Boeing to buy it.

That is the emotion-generating aspect of vision, and this is what is meant by a *compelling* vision. And it is this inspirational component that is so often missing in projects—and entire organizations for that matter.

In a personal communication to me, Mulally wrote:

> *The key message of "Denver to Honolulu on a hot day" for all of us was that we were about something very special—and very hard to do—to create a new airplane that could actually do this mission, which is a tremendous technical feat, and do it reliably day after day and provide great service to the passengers and the airlines.*
>
> *"Denver to Honolulu on a hot day" was about who we were and what we could do together—if we pulled together all of the needed skills: program management, engineering, manufacturing, human resources, communications, finance, marketing, sales, services, contracts, legal, our suppliers, our customers, our investors, the media, and* every employee—and *worked together to find a way to help each other to create and deliver and support a very special and valuable product and service.*
>
> *"Denver to Honolulu on a hot day" and* working together *changed our lives. We are all different. We want more of creating special things and creating a very special environment, so as many people as possible have the opportunity to grow and experience the true satisfaction that can only come from meaningful accomplishment—and have so much fun (emphasis added).*

To illustrate that Mulally was able to create this excitement with what seems to be a simple slogan, Walt Gillette, who was chief project engineer for airplane performance, safety, and reliability on the 777 program, wrote me the following email:

The statement, "Denver to Honolulu on a hot day" meant all the following:

- ❑ It was very visual—in our mind's eye, we could imagine ourselves as the captain and first officer of this flight, seeing the heat waves rising off the concrete runway in the thin air of Denver, and having full confidence that our silver machine would take us safely into the air.

- □ "Denver" meant that the airplane had the high-altitude capability from the onset to do this difficult mission.
- □ "Hot day" meant that the airplane had gone into revenue service in the summer, as promised five years earlier.
- □ "Honolulu" meant that the airplane had ETOPS ability at the start of revenue service.

These images in the minds of the 777 creation team evoked by "Denver to Honolulu on a hot day" spoke to the heart in a way that facts and data could not. Each of us was able to internalize what our share of the assignment meant to achieving this vision (Personal correspondence. Used by permission).

As I have already said, people want meaning in their lives. They want to be part of something important—something that makes a difference in the world, that touches the lives of other people. It is one thing to design an airplane. It is quite another to design the *world's best airplane!*

Tom Peters wrote about this recently when he talked about the WOW project (Peters, 1999). He suggested that project managers must convey the importance and excitement of the project to their team. And if it isn't important, why are we doing it?

Furthermore, if you as the project manager aren't excited about the project, why should it turn anyone else on? You can't sell anything that you don't believe in.

MacMillan and McGrath talk about the importance of vision and leadership in an article in the *London Financial Times*. "The business proposition for a corporate venture needs to have three properties:

- ❏ It must be simple.
- ❏ It must be actionable.
- ❏ It must resonate with people.

"When it comes to simplicity, managers should ask themselves whether they can write it on a business card and still convey its purpose. This makes the business proposition easy to comprehend and communicate. The proposition for Canon's personal copier exemplifies this principle: 'Take to market a copier that is small, inexpensive and reliable enough for personal use on a secretary's desk.' And the Japanese music equipment manufacturer Yamaha replaced the idea of being a company that only manufactured pianofortes with the terse proposition: 'Sell keyboards.'" (MacMillan and McGrath, 2000, p. 12). Notice that Mulally's "Denver to Honolulu on a hot day" conforms very nicely to this requirement of simplicity, and also was actionable and resonated with people.

WHAT IF THE PROJECT ISN'T VERY EXCITING?

There can be no doubt that not all projects can be world-class in nature. But if the project is worth doing, it must be important, and the project manager's job is to help members of the team understand why the job is important. What will it do for the company (besides improving the bottom-line)? Who outside the company will benefit from it? What's in it for the members of the team—that is, what kinds of tangible and intangible rewards will they derive from their contribution in the job? (If there is nothing in it for them, why do you have them on the team? Perhaps you should find someone else.)

One mistake made by scores of project managers or their organizations is to assign people to projects simply because they have the skills or—worse yet—they happen to be available, but with no regard to whether their needs will be met through participation in the project. Then they try to motivate those individuals to do work that is not right for them. This is solving the wrong problem. I know it is not always possible to assign the right person every time—the right person may be unavailable. But we need to understand that you can't motivate people to do jobs that have no inherent characteristics to provide the person with motivation.

Leading, Not Managing

It is common practice to refer to leaders and managers as being one and the same, yet we all know that many of our managers are definitely not leaders. Vance Packard defined leadership as "The art of getting others to want to do something that you are convinced should be done" (Packard, 1962). I believe the operative word in this definition is *want*. A leader is someone who knows how to get people to go beyond compliance.

> *Leadership is the art of getting people to want to do something you are convinced should be done.*
>
> —**Vance Packard**

They actually want to do what the leader suggests. On the other hand, a guard over a prison work crew gets them to do useful work, but it is through coercion or compliance, rather than motivation.

The word *manage* comes from an old French word that originally had the meaning of "handling horses." And, while some people use the word interchangeably with leadership, it more appropriately applies to the administrative aspects of the job. As Warren Bennis has written

> *To survive in the 21ˢᵗ century, we're going to need a new generation of leaders—leaders, not managers.*
>
> *The distinction is an important one. Leaders conquer the context—the volatile, turbulent, ambiguous surroundings that sometimes seem to conspire against us and will surely suffocate us if we let them—while managers surrender to it. There are other differences, as well, and they are critical:*
>
> ❏ *The manager administers; the leader innovates.*

- *The manager is a copy; the leader is an original.*
- *The manager maintains; the leader develops.*
- *The manager focuses on systems and structure; the leader focuses on people.*
- *The manager relies on control; the leader inspires trust.*
- *The manager has a short-range view; the leader has a long-range perspective.*
- *The manager asks how and when; the leader asks what and why.*
- *The manager has his eye on the botttom line; the leader has his eye on the horizon.*
- *The manager accepts the status quo; the leader challenges it.*
- *The manager is the classic good soldier; the leader is his own person.*
- *The manager does things right; the leader does the right thing (Bennis, 2000, p. 5).*

Bennis has spent the last ten years talking with leaders, including Jim Burke at Johnson & Johnson, John Scully at Apple Computer, television producer Norman Lear, and about 100 other men and women. He says, ". . . every leader I talked with shared at least one characteristic: a concern with a guiding purpose, an overarching vision . . . I think of it this way: *Leaders manage the dream.* All leaders have the capacity to create a compelling vision, one that takes people to a new place, and the ability to translate that vision into reality" (Bennis, 2000, p. 6).

> *Leaders manage the dream.*
> —Warren Bennis

There is a caution offered by Zander and Zander in their book, *The Art of Possibility.* Ben Zander, who conducts the Boston Philharmonic Orchestra, says, "A conductor can be easily seduced by the public's extraordinary attention to his unique offering and come to believe that he is personally superior. . . . Yet in the music business, as in all walks of life, a leader who feels he is superior is likely to suppress the voices of the very people on whom he must rely to deliver his vision alive and kicking" (p. 67). In other words, a small dose (or maybe a large one) of humility is needed by every leader to keep from thinking that he or she *is* the team! Ben Zander goes on to say, "I had been conducting for nearly twenty years when it suddenly dawned on me that the conductor of an orchestra *does not make a sound!*. . . his true power derives from his ability to make other people powerful" (p. 68, emphasis added).

The Nature of the Vision

People are not inspired by a higher net margin. They are not inspired by increased market share. And they are not inspired—at least not for very long—by a bigger paycheck. None of these things will cause them to achieve extraordinary goals or superior levels of performance.

> *Something to believe in will.*
> *A leader's first job is to articulate a clear, compelling vision for his organization. What does this enterprise stand for? What does it believe in? And where is it going? The best leaders know that a vision with a single voice never amounts to much. So they share the vision across the organization, enlisting the input and participation of all employees. By letting everyone shape the vision, the leader inspires people and builds commitment (Rosen, 1996, p. 29).*

The reality, as Karl Albrecht writes, is that, "A remarkable number of firms seem to have only the vaguest sense of their own identity and uniqueness. Many don't really know who they are." He goes on to say, "In twenty years of working with organizations of almost every imaginable type, I've seen relatively few really powerful and meaningful corporate statements of vision, mission, or philosophy" (Albrecht, 1994, p. viii).

In the seminars that I have taught since 1980, I have many times asked people to tell me the mission of their company. Most are unable to do so. However, I say, "Well, I can tell you what it is." They always look surprised. Then I say, "More than likely, your mission statement says something like, 'Our mission is to produce world-class stuff that will make a lot of money for our stockholders.'" They all laugh and agree that this is true.

As Rosen has said, such statements do not inspire the people who must make it happen. We forget that organizations are people. At the end of the day, when everyone goes home, the capital equipment and real estate don't make you any money—it's the people who do! And continuing with Albrecht's observations, "Most executive teams have trouble articulating the driving success premise of their enterprises, not because they can't compose flowery phrases, but because they don't *have* a driving premise . . . People in such organizations merely work for a living, not for a higher purpose" (Albrecht, p. ix).

Creating a Vision that Inspires

If you find your company's vision uninspiring, here are some questions suggested by Warren Bennis that may help give it color and dimension:

- ❏ What is unique about us?
- ❏ What values are true priorities for the next year?
- ❏ What would make me professionally commit my mind and heart to this vision over the next five to ten years?
- ❏ What does the world really need that our company can and should provide?
- ❏ What do I want our company to accomplish so that I will be committed, aligned and proud of my association with the institution? (Bennis, 2000, pp. 10–11).

IDEALIZED DESIGN OF THE FUTURE

There are two ways to think about the future of an organization. One is to assume that the world will be a certain way and to try to place the organization's future design in that context. However, there is no ready-made, already-defined future out there waiting for us to arrive at it. The future that will exist when we get there will be the one that we have collectively created by the decisions and actions we take every day between now and then. So we may as well ask ourselves, "What do we want the future to be?" and then pursue the creation of it.

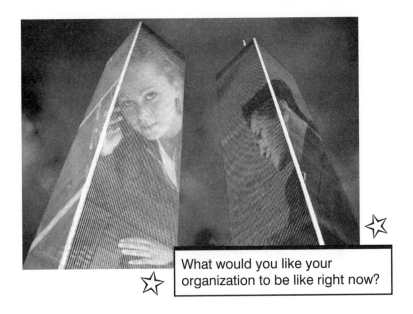

What would you like your organization to be like right now?

Russell Ackoff (1981, 1994) calls this *idealized design*. But he differs slightly from many authors in his approach to it. Most future design processes have you place yourself in the future and ask what it should be like. Ackoff suggests that a different approach is to ask yourself what you would really like the ideal organization to be *right now*! This is a subtle difference, but one that is important. It removes the hang-ups that some people experience when they project themselves into the future and start wondering what things will be like.

Once you have developed a model for the ideal *present*, you contrast it with present reality and then you understand the gap that must be closed. Yes, it will probably take some time to close that gap, and the steps you take may be impeded by unexpected environmental events, but this procedure helps avoid the paralysis that people sometimes experience by worrying too much about things they can't anticipate or control.

To deal with the unexpected events, Ackoff suggests that you identify some of the possibilities and develop contingency plans to cope with them. That way, should they occur, you will be prepared.

One of the techniques used in idealized design is to tell everyone to forget any obstacles that they may think of as they go through the design. Go for broke! Make it the way you would really like it to be. You can always come down from the ideal, but you will find that it can be hard to go up from some lesser model.

<table><tr><td>

Forget reality! Go for broke!
</td></tr></table>

The power in this approach is that this idealized design is not created by a planning team, or even by the senior management team. Rather, it is created by the entire organization, through the process of representation. As Ackoff has pointed out, a democracy is one in which every member has some input to decisions that concern him (or her). This is clearly impossible once a group gets very large. The founding fathers of the United States recognized this, and designed our political system as a *representative democracy,* one in which the citizens elect their representatives. It is this system that Ackoff advocates in large organizations.

I have conducted a number of future search conferences, and can say without hesitation that it is one of the most powerful approaches for generating energy, involvement, and ultimately *commitment!* By involving everyone in the design process, you get all kinds of ideas that you couldn't possibly think of if you were limited to a small management group or planning team. You also get buy-in from the people who participated in the design. Then, when you begin to implement the design, you find that it goes much better than traditional approaches in which a design is "laid on" the organization by senior managers.

What is amazing about the process is the energy it generates. Most workshops last from two to two and a half days, and they are highly structured by the facilitator, in the sense that the group is kept working full-time for the duration of the workshop. When possible, two facilitators are present to help the groups with group process. One such workshop—the first one I ever conducted, in fact—was with the principals and superintendent of a school system. At the end of the program, we sat around debriefing, and one of the principals said, "You know, I just realized something. Ordinarily, if I had worked as hard as I have today, I would be exhausted. I'm not. I feel really up!"

As I watched, I could see the expressions on their faces change as one by one they all came to the same conclusion. And every such workshop that I have conducted since that first one has ended the same way. Weisbord (1987, 1992) says that this is because the normal approach to dealing with situations is to treat it as problem-solving. Such sessions have been tape-recorded, and an interesting thing is observed. As time goes by, energy declines. You can hear it in people's voices, which trail off, leaving sentences unfinished. You also hear frustration as they unsuccessfully cope with whatever problem faces them. Creating something, on the other hand, is energizing.

The other fascinating thing about these workshops is the consensus they develop. When you are dealing with a group of from 30 to 150 individuals, you can't keep them together in one large group. Instead, you break them into small teams of perhaps seven to nine, with as much diversity as you can get, and you have each group design the ideal organization. To tap into their creativity, you tell them that they must present their design in the form of a skit, song, play, or whatever, but it can't be just a boring lecture. You also tell them that every member must participate in the presentation. They don't necessarily need to talk, but they must participate. This frees those with stage fright from having to struggle with a presentation.

Now the amazing thing is that when they start presenting, you would almost swear that they colluded in their design process. There is so much commonality between the groups that it is uncanny. And the differences that do exist get rolled into the final design if the entire group decides to do so.

For more on how these workshops are conducted, you may want to consult Weisbord's book *Common Ground* (1992), Weisbord and Janoff's *Future Search* (1995), and Bunker and Alban's book *Large Group Interventions* (1997).

QUESTIONS TO ANSWER

Each of the eleven principles raises questions that must be answered by every manager in implementing a Working Together program. Here are a few that you should consider.

- ❏ What are we about?
- ❏ What are we going to contribute to the larger good?
- ❏ What difference are we going to make?
- ❏ What contributions will we make?
- ❏ What does success look like?
- ❏ What does it mean to us?
- ❏ What does it mean to me?
- ❏ What is expected of me?
- ❏ Am I proud to be part of this? (Personal correspondence from Alan Mulally. Used by permission.)

A RESOURCE

Joel Barker, the futurist, has produced several videos on the power of paradigms in our lives and our organizations. He has also produced one entitled *The Power of Vision*. You can order it from ChartHouse (800-328-3789). Information on Barker's work can be found on his Web site www.joelbarker.com.

5

You Must Have Clear Performance Goals

THE FOUR PROJECT GOALS

Performance

Cost

Time

Scope

*R*emember that the mission of an organization or a project is to achieve the vision. In the case of the Boeing 777, the mission was to develop an airplane that conformed to the vision of a world-class, technologically superior plane that would fly from Denver to Honolulu on a hot day. The mission can, in turn, only be achieved if various goals and objectives are reached. These goals must be clear to everyone and must be committed to by the people who must accomplish them. I would add that the goals must not only be clear but also should not be conflicting. As we shall see, this is a principle that is often violated.

Although it may seem obvious, you cannot develop goals unless you first have a clear mission and vision, although we often see it happen. Because of the tendency to suboptimize organizations by trying to improve the accounting department, for exam-

PRINCIPLE: You must have clear performance goals.

ple, you will see goals set for accounting that conflict with the goals of other departments. This is the main reason why overall planning for a company must be done as a coordinated effort, rather than piecemeal, as we will discuss in Chapter 6.

MANAGING FOR VALUE AND CONFLICTING GOALS

Shortly after I returned from attending the Business Plan Review meeting, I received an email from Jim Jamieson, executive vice president of Commercial Airplane Programs, suggesting that I discuss managing for value and how the principles can achieve that objective. The following are some observations on how managing for value relates to the principles (or vice versa).

> *Value: The wealth created for a company's stockholders through price appreciation and dividends.*

James Knight, in his book *Value Based Management*, defines value creation as "the wealth created for a company's stockholders through price appreciation and dividends" (1998, p. 21). To define value more concretely, Young and O'Byrne say, "To create value for their shareholders, companies must earn returns on invested capital that exceed the cost of that capital" (2001, p. 4). They go on to say that investors have always cared about stock returns, but major changes have taken place in the United States during the past twenty years that have made investors and managers rethink the subject of value.

The trouble is, says Knight, "Today's managers are receiving conflicting signals, signals that prevent the company from achieving its full potential . . . these conflicting signals [come] from the performance measures used in each of the management

> *Today's managers are receiving conflicting signals about goals, because management processes are not aligned.*

processes, including strategic planning, budgeting, reporting, and compensation . . . These signals conflict with one another because the management processes are not aligned. Strategic planning emphasizes one goal or objective, while the budgeting process emphasizes another, and the incentive system rewards a third. A common conflict is a strategic planning process that emphasizes growth, while the annual budget is focused on earnings per share. Is it any wonder managers are confused?" (op cit., p. 1).

In my experience with project managers, I have found that there is frequently a conflict between project goals and operating goals. This is especially true when a project must draw resources from several divisions of a corporation, as frequently happens. The division manager is measured for achieving operational goals, usually defined as shipping so much product per month and meeting certain financial targets.

When a project manager needs resources from that division and sharing those people affects the division manager's ability to meet her targets, she naturally resists giving them up. The result is that the project then can't be successful, and the project manager, who is at the mercy of line managers for his resources, is between a rock and a hard place. All he can do is appeal to a higher authority to intervene, since he has no leverage over the division manager.

The solution to these problems, says Knight, is to adopt the mind-set of managing for value. This allows managers to prioritize each of their initiatives in the context of the company's goal of creating shareholder value. This mind-set is reflected in the way decisions are made, the way resources are used, and in the rewards earned by managers.

> *The solution to the conflicting goal problem is to adopt a mind-set of managing for value.*

"If a company is managing for value, the company's goal is to deliver value to investors. This does not imply that the company is managed for value to the detriment or exclusion of the customer, the employees, or other important constituents. In fact,. . . the reverse is true. Managing a company for value requires delivering maximum return to the investors while balancing the interests of other important constituents, including customers and employees" (op cit., p. 4).

Knight says that, "over time, consistency is more important and beneficial to shareholders than one-time, value-creating events such as restructuring, financial engineering, and reengineering. . . . The consistent [value-creating] performers created value by improving the operations of their business, becoming more competitive, and grow-

> *Consistency over time is more important and beneficial to shareholders than one-time value-creating actions such as restructuring.*

ing" (op cit., pp. 50–51). To prove this, Knight cites a study of the Standard and Poors 500 population that shows that "one-time value creators created, on average, 62 percent of value relative to their peers. The consistent value creators, on the other hand, created 400 percent of the value of their peers" (op cit., p. 51).

PRESSURE ON GOLIATHS

Goliath automaker GM is feeling the pressure to create value for their shareholders. In an article in the *Wall Street Journal*, Gregory White wrote,

Last week's moves to kill the 103-year-old Oldsmobile name, cut 15,000 jobs and shutter 15% of GM's factory capacity in Europe are only the first steps in the most sweeping overhaul since the dark days of the early 1990s, when losses at the company's bloated North American operations nearly tilted GM into collapse.

GM is nowhere near a financial crisis now. But as the global auto industry braces for its first significant slowdown in six years, GM's 47-year-old leader is under pressure to move faster to boost the company's mediocre profit margins and give investors a better return on the billions GM plows into its core business each year (White, 2000, p. 1).

HOW DO YOU MEASURE PERFORMANCE?

A major issue for companies trying to manage for value is in how they measure performance. Traditionally, the measures have been almost exclusively financial. They have not included an assessment of human resources. This is changing. Writing in the *London Financial Times*, Christopher Ittner and David Larcker say, "A recent survey of US financial services companies found most were not satisfied with their measurement systems. They believed there was too much emphasis on financial measures such as earnings and accounting returns and little emphasis on drivers of value such as customer and employee satisfaction, innovation and quality. In response, companies are implementing new performance measurement systems . . . [such as] . . . 'intangible assets' and 'intellectual capital' to 'balanced scorecards' of integrated financial and non-financial measures" (Ittner and Larcker, 2000, p. 8).

Performance measures must go beyond purely financial numbers.

To succeed at managing value, companies must understand their value drivers, those factors that create stakeholder value. Most companies do a poor job at this, say Ittner and Larcker. "For example, many executives rate environmental performance and quality as relatively unimportant drivers of long-term financial performance. In contrast, statistical analyses indicate these dimensions are strongly associated with a company's market value" (op cit., p. 10).

Performance Goals in Projects

It is the project manager's job to make sure every contributor knows three things: *what* must be done, *by when* it must be done, and *how acceptable performance will be measured.* Note that it is not his or her concern with how the person will do the work. That is the expert's responsibility to work out. Of course, in a very large project the project manager must depend on team leaders of various functions to ensure that individual contributors have clear performance goals, but unless he has established these for the team leaders, they cannot be passed down to individual contributors.

In addition, each person must know the limits of his or her authority, responsibility, and accountability. You cannot delegate responsibility without delegating authority commensurate with it.

The Four Project Goals

In every project there are four goals that must be met. These are called performance, cost, time, and scope (P, C, T, S), and they are interdependent, as we will see later on.

Performance Performance relates to what the deliverable is supposed to do. How must it perform? The 777 is supposed to carry a certain number of passengers and cargo from Denver to Honolulu on a hot day. It should fly at a certain altitude, burn so many gallons of fuel per hour, and so on. The airplane was also supposed to have an empty weight of only so many pounds. If that target were not met, Boeing would have to pay United Airlines so many dollars per flight mile, because the fuel efficiency would not be as high as specified. [As a bit of trivia, the airplane weighed in within a few hundred pounds of the target! This is an incredible accomplishment in itself, given the enormous complexity of the product (see Sabbagh, 1995)].

THE FOUR PROJECT GOALS

Performance

Cost

Time

Scope

Cost Cost is the total cost to do the project. If a project is justified by assuming a certain return on investment (ROI) and the investment is greater than planned, then the ROI will not be met. Thus, cost control is very important in almost all projects, although it is not always the most important one.

Time Rather, it is often time that is the most important target in many contemporary projects. Boeing promised United Airlines that the first 777 would be delivered in May 1995. The airline in turn planned flight schedules, promotion of their new airplane, and crew training based on Boeing's promised delivery. If Boeing was either early or late, this would create a problem for the airline. Early delivery would mean that the airline might not be prepared to pay the bill. Late delivery might mean canceling a scheduled flight (at considerable loss of revenue).

It is typical that the time frame is highly critical. With new products, the first company to market usually gets as much as 70 percent of market share, and it becomes difficult for later entries to take that position from the leader. So speed is life in today's world, and this is the one variable or goal that can be most affected by good project management.

Some years ago, Hewlett-Packard found that if they were one month late to market with a new computer, they might lose one-third of total product sales. They also determined that they could justify spending as much as 25 percent more on the project than originally planned, as long as they met the target date, and this would only affect their net profits by a few percentage points (Patterson, 1993).

Scope Scope is the size or magnitude of the job. The 777 involved developing several million new parts, only some of which were designed by Boeing. The engines, for example, were actually designed and built by General Electric, Rolls Royce, and Pratt-Whitney. So a scope statement for development of the 777 would exclude design of the engines. The program manager would, of course, have responsibility for seeing that the engine development projects were coordinated with such things as wing design, which was done by Boeing. Otherwise you may end up with an engine that won't mount properly on the wing, or a wing that won't properly support the weight and stresses placed on it by the engine.

It is a fact of life that one major cause of project failures is that scope tends to grow. This can happen because people forget something in the planning stage, because unforeseen things develop, or because something in the environment changes and the team must respond to the change. As an example of the environmental factor, advances in technology can cause a change in scope. Since the 777 was supposed to be one of the most technologically advanced planes ever built, if a vendor were to develop a new, extremely sophisticated, wind-shear warning device, Boeing would most likely want to incorporate that device in their airplane, even though they had planned to use a less sophisticated one originally. That decision could require major design changes to the already completed area of the flight deck. But it might be such a desirable change that it would be made regardless of the impact to the project.

You Can't Dictate All Four Goals

The most important thing to understand about the four goals of a project is that you cannot arbitrarily assign values to all four of them. They

You can't dictate all four goals—one has to float.

are interrelated. The general expression that relates them is:

$$C = f(P, T, S)$$

which reads, "Cost is a function of Performance, Time, and Scope."

The cost component in this equation is labor costs only. Material and capital equipment costs do not enter into the direct relationship with the others. They are important to the overall cost of the project, however, but they must be tracked in a separate budget from labor costs.

Now suppose the P, T, and S targets are dictated by job requirements. The project manager then estimates what resources she needs to meet the targets on the right side of the equation, which in turn equate with labor costs. In many cases, when she tells the project sponsor the cost figure, it is higher than expected. In fact, the sponsor may say that the company can't afford the price stated by the project manager.

The response must be, "Then you tell me what you can afford, and I'll tell you what I can give you for it." This is not an insubordinate response. It is a reality. If you can only afford a certain number of dollars, we may be able to reduce scope to a level that will cost what you can afford, and that scope level may still yield a suitable result. If it does not, then we may be able to extend time a little and reduce costs. If none of these work, then the only remaining option would be to change the process by which the work is done to improve work efficiency, which would reduce costs or force us to forgo the project.

Pressures to Reduce Both Time and Cost

Most companies are feeling enormous market pressures to get their projects done both faster and cheaper. The difficulty is, there is a time-cost tradeoff, as shown in Figure 5.1, such that, if you try

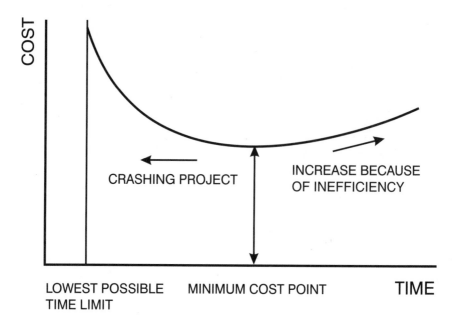

COST

CRASHING PROJECT

INCREASE BECAUSE
OF INEFFICIENCY

LOWEST POSSIBLE   MINIMUM COST POINT   **TIME**
TIME LIMIT

Figure 5.1
The time-cost tradeoff curve for a project.

to reduce time beyond the optimum level shown on the curve, you have to spend more money to do it. Note also that the increase in cost is very nonlinear, because you usually speed up a project by throwing more resources at it, and this leads to inefficiencies, so that the time-cost tradeoff is never linear.

So how are you going to reduce both time and cost? There is only one way—you must change the process by which the work is done. For the 777 program, the design process was changed. Rather than using traditional two-dimensional design methods, Boeing switched to three-dimensional computer design throughout, which reduced rework and eliminated many of the hardware tests that would normally have to be done—instead, computer simulation was used to prove concepts.

If you always do what you've always done, you'll always get what you always got.

No matter what kind of project you are dealing with, the PCTS constraints affect all of them. You are always making tradeoffs among them. As a project manager, you must be able to show

When continuous measures like weight, length, time, or pressure are possible, it is easy to tell if a goal has been met.

stakeholders how those tradeoffs work, so that informed decisions can be made based on data, not guesswork.

Metrics

Unless you have a way to measure whether a goal has been achieved, setting it is meaningless. Note that the word *measure* is used in a very broad sense. There are some outcomes that are simply binary—either they have occurred or they have not. In that case, the metric is a check mark on a checklist.

When continuous measures like weight, length, time, or pressure are possible, it is easy to tell if a goal has been met. When the goal is something like improved morale or customer satisfaction, it is more difficult to measure and therefore we will be less certain if a target has been achieved.

In either case, the metric that tells whether a goal has been reached is called an *exit criteria*. You are finished and can go on to something else. Sometimes the exit criteria will be an approval by an individual. The customer, for example, signs a document saying that he or she is satisfied with what has been done, and thus that you have met the target. Other times, the exit criteria may be qualitative—a stakeholder agrees that one dress style is more attractive than another.

You must have performance goals tied to some kind of exit criteria that indicate that the goal has been met, or you will never be able to get closure on project work.

Keep It Simple

Patrick Shanahan started with Boeing in the Defense Business Sector, but transferred to Commercial during the 777 development program. He was educated as an engineer, but took a job as a first-line supervisor. In a phone interview he told me that Mulally has a way of stating goals in such a way that they promote the right behavior, the right interactions, and so that people don't misunderstand. This is essential when not everyone can have the big picture, no matter how much communication takes place. But by expressing goals in the right way, everyone can connect. This is how large-scale system integration is achieved.

First there was the vision (and goal, if you consider that the mission is to achieve the vision) of developing a plane that would fly from Denver to Honolulu on a hot day. This conveyed something of the technical requirements to those Boeing employees who understood the implications. It also gave even nontechnical people some idea—it's a long way from Denver to Honolulu—and much of it is over water. And it will only have two engines. What if one of them quits? Well, we can't have that happening very often, can we, so those engines better be darned good! And big! Yes, the diameter of a single engine is as large as the entire fuselage (body) of a 737, which will carry about 125 passengers. Man, does that give you an idea of the size of that thing? Such is the power of this simple statement.

But Alan went beyond that statement. He also told everyone that the 777 had to be delivered on time, be service ready—meaning ready to fly people over water—right "out of the box." This theme was repeated over and over again, so that every mechanic, engineer, or assembler understood it. It formed a vivid vision in their minds and conveyed the level of responsibility that they had in their jobs. They were building an airplane that would carry people over water, and it had to do so as soon as it left the factory.

QUESTIONS TO ANSWER

As I said in the previous chapter, here are some questions you should consider in developing your Working Together program.

- ❑ What are our goals?
- ❑ How will we measure them?
- ❑ Does moving forward and making progress on our goals and measures move us closer to our vision?
- ❑ Are our goals and measures comprehensive enough? (Personal correspondence from Alan Mulally. Used by permission.)

6

One Plan

E ver since my first book, which was published in 1991, I have been emphasizing that you must have a plan if you are going to run projects (or organizations) successfully. My argument has always been based on the definition of control:

> Control is exercised by comparing where you are to where you are supposed to be so you can take corrective action to get back on track when you have a deviation.

Given that the plan tells where you are supposed to be, it follows that, if you have no plan, you don't know where you are supposed to be, so control is impossible. I have often summed this up by saying, "No plan, no control," and one of my clients took me seriously and bought shirts for their employees with this slogan embroidered on them.

PRINCIPLE: You've got to have a plan.

Not only must you have a plan in order to have control, but because an organization is a social system in which the parts interact, you must have an *integrated* plan, not a hodgepodge of individual department plans that don't hang together. (This will be discussed in more detail later in this chapter.) Yet a study by Henry Mintzberg, in which he shadowed senior managers, found that few of them do any systematic planning. And, while I agree that this is how it is, I am afraid his findings tend to validate the idea for many managers that, since other managers don't do it and they are successful, then there is no need for me to do it. This is not meant as a criticism of Mintzberg's study. It is, however, an indictment of those who will conclude what they already believed by ignoring the real meaning of the findings.

Anyone who concludes that because most managers don't plan means that planning is unnecessary is making a fatal mistake, in my opinion. I believe that many organizations are successful *in spite* of themselves, rather than *because of* themselves. The reason I say this is that they often have good products and services that

If you have no plan, you have no control—by definition!

they can sell at large enough profit margins to cover the sloppiness of the day-to-day mismanagement of the business.

I base this conclusion on my own experience in consulting and training, where I have had thousands of seminar participants lament about how things are done where they work, leading me to be-

Many organizations are successful in spite of themselves, rather than because of themselves.

lieve that in some companies, as someone has said, "The first myth of management is that it exists." I don't believe that this is universally true, of course. There are some well-managed companies. But even after Tom Peters and Bob Waterman wrote their ground-breaking book *In Search of Excellence*, they found several years later that many of the companies they had included in their book as examples of excellence had slid off the cliff (Peters and Waterman, 1982).

A major reason, I believe is, as Knight has said, ". . . management processes are not aligned" (Knight, 1998, p. 1), and because, as Karl Albrecht has written, "Most executive teams have trouble articulating the driving success premise of their enterprises . . . because they don't *have* a driving premise" (Albrecht, 1994, pp. viii–ix). A proper plan cannot be developed under such conditions, so it may be that this is actually the reason for the dearth of planning in management, rather than sloth.

THE FUNCTION OF MANAGEMENT

If the function of management is to ensure that an organization not only survives but creates value for its stakeholders, as I have discussed in Chapter 5, then that suggests a need to have some control over what the organization does. And that control cannot be achieved without a plan that is tied to a clear vision, mission, and sound performance goals—by definition. I believe that Mintzberg's finding can be explained also by the fact that many managers spend most of their time fighting fires, so that they

The function of management is to ensure that an organization not only survives, but creates value for its stakeholders.

never find the time to do any real planning. Ironically, many of those fires exist because these very managers had no plan to start with, meaning that they had no control. This creates a vicious circle, from which there is no escape except to somehow make the time for planning.

THE HIGH COST OF NOT PLANNING

The need for planning is supported by the annual Standish Group studies. They began surveying software development projects and published one of their studies in 1994. That study found that we spent some $250 billion on software development in the United States that year, and only 17 percent of those projects met their original targets. Another 50 percent of the software projects had to have the targets revised. That is, they were late, over budget, had reduced functionality, and so on. Incredibly, the remaining 33 percent were canceled! This means that nearly $80 billion were wasted on canceled software projects.

Furthermore, when asked what were the major correlates with success, the respondents said that *good planning* and good understanding of customer requirements were the two top factors! (For a free copy of one of their reports, check out their Web site: www.standishgroup.com.)

I believe that we will find similar statistics for product development projects in general. For example, Mulally has estimated that nearly 30 percent of the cost to develop a new airplane is rework. As he puts it, that is equivalent to having one of every three engineers working full time on the project to just redo what the other two engineers did wrong in the first place. On a $5 billion project, that's a lot of wasted shekels! Again, the high rework is attributed to poor planning.

Harry and Schroeder (2000), authors of one of the first books on Six-Sigma programs, have stated that most organizations in the United States are running at about a three-sigma quality level. They say that the cost of poor quality at this level is from 25 to 40 percent of every dollar in sales. Phil Crosby, former vice president of quality at ITT, and inventor of the Zero Defects concept, says that cost of poor quality falls into three categories: prevention, appraisal, and failure. Prevention is the cost to keep errors from happening in the first place. Appraisal is the inspection we do to find the errors that have been made. And failure is the cost of warranty that we incur when errors get to the customer and must be corrected.

> *Most organizations operate at a three-sigma quality level. For every million opportunities to screw up, they will do so 66,400 times.*

To put it into perspective, a three-sigma quality level means that for every million opportunities we have to do something wrong, we will do it wrong 66,400 times. At the six-sigma level, that number of errors drops to 3.4 in a million opportunities, and the cost of poor quality drops to a few pennies for each dollar of sales.

MISINTERPRETATION OF SCIENCE

More justification for not planning has in recent years been derived from an interpretation of findings in chaos theory. Chaos theory suggests that if a butterfly flaps its wings in California, the effect will be felt on the East Coast very soon. The idea is that small amounts of turbulence in the environment lead to large effects, and this has been taken to mean that there is therefore no need to plan very far out because these effects will make your plans obsolete almost as fast as they are made.

That may be true in the longer term, and if planning is done as usual, I agree that long-range planning should only be done in very broad brush strokes. Short-term planning, however, should be done in more detail if an organization is to be in control at all.

AMERICAN CULTURE COMPARED TO OTHERS

I was recently told about a study of how children perform tasks that is instructive in understanding why Americans don't do a better job of planning.[1] Children from Japan, Germany, and the United States took part in the study. The children were all given a Lego toy to assemble. The box was still sealed when the children received it.

The Japanese children opened the box, took out the instructions, read them carefully, and then assembled the toy. The German children removed the parts, grouped them into piles of similar shapes and colors, then read the instructions, and assembled their toy. The American children ripped open the box, tossed the instructions to the side, and began to assemble the toy from the picture on the box. They finished with parts left over. The Japanese and German children had no parts left over, and their toys were exactly like they were supposed to be.

This study shows that we Americans learn to take a Ready-Fire-Aim approach to our work at a fairly early age. We would rather take action than plan. And certainly there are times when this is the best thing to do. However, it is not true most of the time, and it is almost never true in projects.

---

1. I would be indebted to any reader who can tell me the source of this study. Write me at jlewis@lewisinstitute.com.

DIFFERENT STROKES FOR DIFFERENT FOLKS

What should vary is not *whether* you plan but the level of detail that you include in the plan. I have been told many times by scientists that you can't plan research projects. This is absolutely not true. What they are confused about is that there are conditional branches in such projects. They are going to do a study, and, depending on the outcome of that study, they may go in one direction or another. Fine. You can still plan up to that conditional branch, and once you reach it, you plan the next stage. We call this approach *phased* planning, or sometimes it is called a *rolling* plan.

This approach is often appropriate in poorly defined work. Even long-duration software projects may have an evolutionary nature. Highsmith (2000) has written that many software programs are adaptive. They must adapt to changes that take place in the environment while they are being done or you won't have a viable product when you finish. Of course, this is often true of hardware development projects as well, and the danger is that you will never release the product if you continuously change it. Someone in the organization must make a decision about when to freeze the specifications and let the revisions be done to the next generation of the product.

OVERCOMING THE RESISTANCE TO PLANNING

There are two basic reasons why people don't want to do project planning. One is that they don't believe it is necessary. I call this the paradigm problem. A *paradigm* is a belief about something, and the belief is tremendously powerful. Once a person believes something to be true, he or she behaves in ways that serve to confirm that belief, thereby never finding that the belief may not be true. I have seen this in project managers who have been around for many years. They have been successful (at least in their own minds) and see no reason to add the burden of planning. It is just

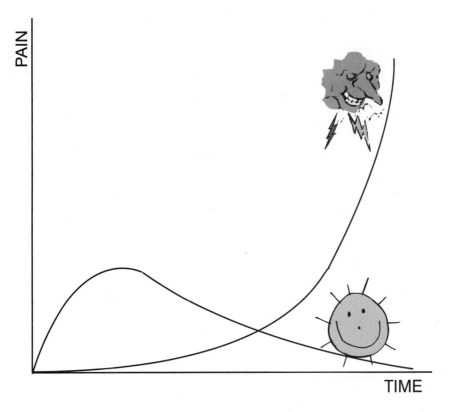

Figure 6.1
Pain curves in a project over time.

extra work to them, and it is very difficult to convince them that there is any reason to add that burden. Usually it simply has to be mandated.

The second most common reason for not planning is that the process inflicts pain on people. It is hard work, no question about it. The consequence of not planning, however, is that pain grows exponentially in a project over time. The two pain curves are shown in Figure 6.1. Most human beings avoid pain, if possible, and definitely want a quick cure for it when it does occur, so when a manager puts them on Curve 1, they rebel against it.

People also avoid planning out of fear of reprisal if they do not meet the targets to which they must commit. Or if they must commit, they simply pad their time estimates so that they are fairly certain that they can meet the dates they have given.

80

Once those dates have been published, you can be sure the work will not be finished earlier than specified. Parkinson's law says that work will always expand to take as long as has been al-lowed. And even if it does not do this—even if a task were finished ahead of time—the person next in line will most likely not start early. Eli Goldratt (1997) calls this the

> *Parkinson's Law: Work will always expand to take the time allowed.*

student effect, and for these two reasons, he says projects will accu-mulate delays but will never accumulate gains.

The term *student effect* comes from the study habits of students in school. The instructor announces on Monday morning that there will be a test on Friday. The students all lament that they are already overloaded with tests and beg that this test be postponed. Under this considerable pressure, the instructor moves the test to the following Friday—a week later. When will the students begin studying for the test? You guessed it! Thursday just before the test. They won't have any more study time than if it had been left in its original slot.

In projects, the student effect takes place when a person hands off work to the next person in line before the drop-dead start time. The person looks at the schedule, concludes that the task does not have to start yet, and puts it aside. Then when he finally starts working on it, there will be unexpected difficulties or it will take longer than expected, and it will now finish late. Had he started when first given the input, the project could have finished on time. So he has accumulated a delay, but has not taken advantage of a gain.

CONCEPTS OF PLANNING

To understand the problem with conventional concepts of plan-ning, we need to return for a moment to how organizations have been viewed. Remember that the earliest view was of the organi-zation as a giant machine, with no purpose of its own. This was later replaced by the view of organization as organism—that is, it did have a purpose of its own, but the inner parts did not. Furthermore, its major purpose was to serve the needs of its owners.

This view has finally given way to that of the organization as a social system, which not only has an overall purpose but also recognizes that the parts that make it up (its human members) also have purposes of their own. We know that for the enterprise to thrive and grow, the purposes of all stakeholders need to be balanced.

We also saw that when the organization was viewed as a machine, the belief was that it could be understood through the methods of scientific reductionist thinking. That is, by understanding the parts, one could understand the whole. That view is totally incorrect when the enterprise is a social system, rather than a machine. You cannot understand how a company works as a whole by understanding the functioning of the maintenance department alone. The subsystems of a larger system *interact,* and it is these interactions that give it the unique properties that differentiate it from other organizations.

This mechanistic view shows up in the way planning is done. As Ackoff has pointed out,

> a corporate plan is seen as a collection of the plans separately prepared for each of the parts of the whole. In contrast, the type of planning proposed here proceeds from a treatment of the whole to the interaction of the parts and then finally to the parts themselves. The justification for doing so arises out of the concept of planning that involves dealing with interdependent problems. . . . In brief, planning is here conceptualized as a participative way of dealing with a set of interrelated problems when it is believed that unless something is done, a desirable future is not likely to occur; and that if appropriate action is taken, the likelihood of such a future can be increased (Ackoff, 1981, p. 52).

THE HOLISTIC PRINCIPLE

Planning in a participative way is called *interactive* planning by Ackoff. To achieve a holistic result, two other principles must be understood. These are the *principle of coordination* and the *principle of integration.* The principle of coordination states that no part of an organization can be planned for effectively if it is planned for independently of any other unit at the same level. This means that all units at the same level should be planned for simultaneously and interdependently.

The reason is that a threat or opportunity that appears in one unit may best be treated in another unit. The fact that we label a problem as a production or marketing problem does not mean that the appropriate way of dealing with it is within that function. Yet most managers tend to think of problems in terms of the unit in which they appear. This would be appropriate if the

> *The principle of coordination states that no part of an organization can be planned for effectively if it is planned for independently of any other unit at the same level.*

parts were independent of each other, but if this were true, they would not be parts of an organization. Therefore, unit problems often derive more from the way that units interact than from their own actions taken independently (Ackoff, 1981).

A simple example here may illustrate why the typical approach fails. Suppose the manufacturing department finds itself with excess capacity because they have recently installed new automation. Then the answer is to lay off the excess workers. Deming and Drucker have both argued that this is wrong. The excess workers should be retained while the business takes advantage of its newly gained productivity increases to grow the business. What this means, however, is that these workers may need to be redeployed—perhaps by training them to repair the new automation equipment. Or sales may need to work harder to generate more orders. Or—and this is thinking outside the box—maybe those excess workers can be contracted out to another company in the area temporarily, at a cost large enough to generate some profits! In any case, the problem may have to be solved outside the department in which it occurs, but this can only be seen by thinking systemically, rather than at the micro level.

The principle of integration states that planning done *independently* at any level of a system cannot be as effective as planning carried out *inter*dependently at all levels. For example, we know that a policy or practice that is established at one level of an enterprise often creates problems at other levels. When this happens, the solution is to deal with the policy or procedure at the level where it was created.

When the principles of coordination and integration are combined, we have the *holistic principle,* which states that the more parts of a system and levels of it that plan simultaneously and interdependently, the better. This concept is in direct opposition to the common practice of independent, sequential planning, whether it be top-down or bottom-up (Ackoff, 1981).

> *The principle of integration states that planning done independently at any level of a system cannot be as effective as planning carried out interdependently at all levels.*

IF YOU DON'T PRACTICE THIS PRINCIPLE, YOU GET MANY PLANS

The tendency to plan in isolation from all other parts of the enterprise exists almost everywhere. This is partly due to our view of the enterprise as a bunch of parts that can do their own "thing" independently of the others. But it may also be the result of not having a clear mission and vision for an organization that is understood and shared by everyone—you get fragmented efforts from every function (another reason why the philosophy of Working Together is so important). When no one knows where you are really trying to go as a company, then they go where *they* think you're going, and fragmentation is the result. It is the role of senior management to develop a master plan for the business, and this plan sets the overall direction for the company.

Once a master plan is established, each function develops a plan that is aligned with the master. This includes operations, engineering, services, public relations, and people. (Boeing no longer calls this department Human Resources.)

When the master plan is created and the individual functional plans are developed, true control can occur.

When the master plan is created and the individual functional plans are developed to coordinate with it, true control of the organization can occur. This control is achieved by monitoring progress against the plan(s) and taking action to deal with deviations that will inevitably exist. At Boeing, this monitoring is reported in a weekly Business Plan Review Meeting. They use a combination of technical and nontechnical reporting to show status. The nontechnical scheme uses colored boxes to report status. A green box means you are on target. Yellow means a deviation is large enough to be of some concern (caution), and red means there is a clear problem. A box that is split in half with yellow on the left and green on the right means the caution has changed to green during the last week—the problem has been resolved. The opposite is true the week the problem develops—the box is split with green on the left and yellow on the right.

When no one knows where you are really trying to go as a company, then they go where they think you're going, and fragmentation is the result.

In Chapter 2, I described one of Boeing's meetings in detail, so I will not do so here. Suffice it to say that the coordinated planning of the organization enables them to all be on "one page" together, and to understand how problems being experienced in one part of the organization may affect other parts, so that remedies can be developed together.

JOINT PROBLEM SOLVING

As an example of how this may work, let's assume that during such a status meeting the People Department (to use Boeing's term—Human Resources for most of us) reports that they are having extreme difficulty recruiting people to fill open requisitions. This is across the board, but the greatest difficulty is in finding workers for manufacturing jobs. Having heard this, those managers in manufacturing know that they may have difficulty meeting targets without asking existing personnel to work overtime. This tells the finance department that they are going to see manufacturing costs increase, which will shrink the company's margins, and this will be of concern to stockholders. The public relations people also know that they may need to put a "spin" on this to deal with stakeholder reactions. It is a good-news, bad-news story. The good news is that business is so good that the company is trying to hire. The bad news is that they can't find enough workers.

Now you may argue that there is no difference in this scenario from any similar problem in any company. In any regular status meeting, everyone would have this same awareness. That is true. The difference is in how they respond. This problem needs to be dealt with by the affected parties *jointly*, not independently. There is the real difference. It is a problem of *coordinating* the actions of all parties so that an overall solution is achieved that works for the enterprise as a whole.

QUESTIONS TO ANSWER

Here are the questions to answer about the principle of one plan.

❑ So . . . what is the plan? Really?

❑ The goals?

❑ The strategy—business, products, services, production, people, etc.?

❑ The resources?

❑ The schedule?

❑ The risks?

❑ The opportunities?

❑ The interdependencies?

❑ What is our current status compared to our plan? Where are we?

❑ What is our plan to get back on plan?

❑ Do we need a different plan?

❑ Are we all together?

❑ Are there items that need special attention before our next business plan review? (Personal correspondence from Alan Mulally. Used by permission.)

7

Everyone Is Included

*Y*ou cannot have successful projects—or organizations—that require the collaboration of thousands of people if you practice exclusionary tactics, treating some people as members of the "in group" and others as sec-
ond-class citizens. There is no room for elitist egos in a pro-ject. Actually, it is the antithe-sis of the Working Together principle. Again, Mulally ex-

You can't practice exclusionary tactics if you want collaboration from people.

emplifies the practice of this idea. His philosophy of Working To-gether was screened on the nose of the first 777, and when you enter his office complex, it is placed prominently on the wall be-hind the two receptionists who greet visitors. Furthermore, you can talk with almost anyone in Boeing, and they will tell you that

PRINCIPLE: Everyone is included. ★

he has time for them. He doesn't think he is too good to talk to a factory worker—even when they are on strike. As I have related previously, during a strike that occurred shortly after he became president, he would get out of his car and talk to the people on the picket line—behavior that caused some anxiety for the security people, but made an indelible impression on Boeing employees. Here was a president who cared about them! That may have counted for more than anything else he could have done.

THE FAILURE OF QUALITY CIRCLES

When American companies finally realized that they had a quality problem in 1980, they hit the panic button. The Japanese were taking big shares of their markets. They already had about 25 percent of the auto market before the big three U.S. automakers woke up, and an even larger share of the entertainment electronics market. Why were Americans buying Japanese products, everyone wondered?

As Americans discovered Deming and the quality processes that he taught the Japanese, companies by the hundreds jumped on the quality improvement bandwagon. Quality became the new corporate religion and within that religion, quality circles became the way of solving problems. Or so everyone said.

But within a few years, most of the hype had ended, and companies that had initially embraced quality circles with enthusiasm had abandoned them, saying they had spent a lot of money and had almost nothing to show for it. Why the crash?

First, there is a basic tenet about how quality circles function, which is that the best place to solve a problem is at the level at which it occurs, by the people who know most about the processes involved in creating the problem. Clearly a factory worker knows more about manufacturing processes than most senior managers, so the factory worker should be in a better position to solve any problems that exist in her area. So the workers are trained in problem identification, problem prioritization (using Pareto analysis), cost/benefit analysis, problem solving methods, and presentation skills. They are also taught something about group process so that their team meetings will run efficiently and effectively.

They then meet on a regular basis (during working hours, or if after work they are paid for their time) to identify and solve problems. Later they present their recommended solutions to senior managers for approval, since many of the solutions require expenditures for capital equipment or other things that the workers are not authorized to spend. If they have done their jobs properly, they show that the solution has a payback in so many months, and management will usually approve the approach, as a positive cost/benefit outcome is easily justified.

In a number of companies, however, the workers could not do cost/benefit analyses because management would not give them cost figures. That information was sensitive, management reasoned. If the workers knew the cost of

> *You can bet that your competitors already know your costs—maybe even better than you do! It's their job to find out. They don't need to get it from your employees.*

doing various things, they might divulge that information to others outside the company and soon their competitors would learn their costs, and that would be bad. Very bad.

Without the cost information, the workers had no idea if a proposed solution to a problem was actually worth implementing. If the solution would cost more than the benefit gained, the answer was certainly "no," but without the information, all they could do was recommend the solution to senior managers who would then decide if the fix was justifiable. In many cases they were told the cost was prohibitive, so the team would go back to work on another problem, feeling that they had completely wasted their time only to be shot down, and another round would begin. After half a dozen such rounds, they were so demoralized that they had no incentive to continue.

For their part, senior managers complained that they weren't getting anything out of this—after having spent considerable sums on training and team meetings. Of course the reason was clear to them. The Japanese were more team-oriented than Americans. It was a cultural thing, and quality circles just didn't work in our highly individualistic society. Such claims were made in ignorance or out of disregard for

At one time the highest-producing plant SONY had was in San Diego, using American workers and Japanese management techniques!

the fact that the highest-producing plant that SONY had at the time was in San Diego—using American workers and Japanese management methods! Not only that, but there were many other U.S. companies that were getting good results with quality circles—but they were the ones that embraced the entire program rather than only paying lip service to it.

HANG YOUR BRAIN ON THE GATE

Faced with this behavior of management, workers became bitter and disillusioned. The experience only confirmed what many of them believed all along—that management really didn't want to hear from them, did not respect them, and saw them only as a means to an end. The fellow who told me that his company had tried every new fad that had been invented also told me that in the twenty years that he had worked in the plant, management had expected him to "hang his brain on the front gate" when he arrived at work. Now that they were trying to employ self-directed work teams, he said, "They expect me to carry the whole load."

Not only were the managers of his division asking for an immediate 180-degree shift in how he did his job, from "do what you're told" to "you decide," but he had no confidence that they were serious, given their past behavior. He was sure that, as soon as the wind shifted direction, they would abandon this program for another. Most importantly, he was afraid that if he suggested something and it didn't work, then they would blame him and his job would be in jeopardy.

In many such instances, the workers were right—management did not want to hear from them. Over the years there has evolved an us-versus-them way of thinking—especially in companies that have strong, militant unions. Unfortunately, once such thinking develops, it is hard to break out of it. The situation is one of continuous conflict, with neither side trusting the other. Communication breaks down, and cooperation is a dirty word.

Unfortunately, what happened was that many American managers tried to apply the "technology" of quality circles without actually changing their attitudes toward workers. They still viewed them in terms of the mechanistic or organic view of the organization as replaceable parts. Even though Herzberg has shown that money is a hygiene factor, which does not motivate if it is taken care of but will *demotivate* if it is not, many managers still believe that the only thing that motivates employees is money. They do not believe that meaning, participation, and self-determination are the real factors that drive almost every person in an organization. Believing this, they naturally do not take seriously the efforts of people in quality circles. I believe this was a major cause of the failures.

> *You can't apply the technology of quality circles and still think of people as expendable and get good results.*

PETER DRUCKER AND JAPANESE MANAGEMENT

Almost everyone knows that Deming, Feigenbaum, and Juran (among many others) were sent to Japan at the end of World War II to help rebuild the country. What is less well known is that Dr. Peter Drucker, considered by many to be the "father" of modern

management thinking, was also part of the team. At that time the Japanese saw these men as their salvation—and they were. Their country was in a shambles. As they started making products for export, the quality was so poor that "Made in Japan" became a sarcasm in America for anything of poor quality. So, as someone has said, "The Japanese read Dr. Drucker's books, and they were naive enough to think that if Drucker said it, we Americans must do it that way, so they followed his advice, and by golly, it worked!" And now, the principles that Drucker espoused in his books that were written back in the 1950s were suddenly being reexported back to us.

> *The Japanese were naive enough to think that Americans must do things the way Dr. Drucker suggested, so they followed his advice, and by golly, it worked!*

GAMES WITHOUT END

Zander and Zander have written, "A monumental question for leaders in any organization to consider is: How much greatness

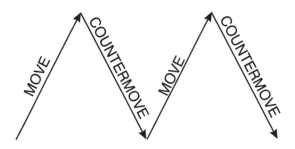

Figure 7.1
The vicious cycle of move-countermove.

are we willing to grant people?" (Zander and Zander, 2000, p. 73). If managers have elitist attitudes, you can bet that the answer will be, "Not very much." When management shows by their actions that they do not have regard for their people, the workers respond by becoming resentful, resisting, and ultimately militant. The relationship between management and labor becomes one of us-versus-them, and this leads to serious problems.

The *interaction* between management and labor now becomes one of move-countermove, and each side sees its own behavior as a response to the behavior of the other side. So, if workers slow down, it is because management has demanded too much of them for the pay that they get. Management says they demand more because the workers weren't performing adequately in the first place, and they were trying to jog them a bit. And on it continues, each side blaming the other for their mutual antagonism. And so it will continue until someone interrupts the pattern. See Figure 7.1.

The Customer Comes Second!

Southwest Airlines CEO Herb Kelleher says that the way you treat your employees is the way they will treat your customers, so if you want to give good customer service, you had better be good to your employees. In fact, at Southwest, the customer comes second—right after the employees (Freiberg and Freiberg, 1996).

> *The way you treat your employees is the way they will treat your customers. You cannot provide good customer service with disgruntled employees.*

The Arms Race as an Example of a Vicious Circle

The arms race that existed between the United States and the Soviet Union is a perfect example of this move-countermove exchange (which is called a *game-without-end*). When Soviet Premier Gorbachev realized that the United States could economically afford to play the game better than the Soviet Union could, he knew he had to end the race. If he continued to escalate his arms buildup, it was going to bankrupt his country. So he did the unthinkable—he started a unilateral *disarmament,* saying to President Reagan, "I'm going to deprive you of an enemy."

It was unthinkable in terms of the mind-set that existed at the time, because the Soviets did see the United States as an adversary. After all, they had been invaded so many times by the Mongols, Germans, and others that they fully believed we might do the same thing. But that unilateral disarmament was a shift from move-countermove to one of no response (or the opposite response to what was expected). Another way to say it is that Gorbachev's response broke the escalation pattern that characterized the interaction. Such behavior is so rare that you seldom see it in real life. Yet it is sometimes the only way out of destructive patterns of behavior.

In order for these games-without-end to exist, each side must view the other as an opponent. This is the ultimate of the competitive stance that turns destructive—each side wants to destroy the other. In a Working Together situation, which also practices the philosophy that Everyone Is Included, that view is difficult for anyone to maintain. It is possible, of course, in such situations as the Middle East, where the hatreds are as ancient as the history of the people themselves. Those who want peace may be in the minority, however. If they ever become the majority, then we may see real peace in that part of the world.

SOME POSITIVE EXAMPLES

In his book, *Moments of Truth,* former SAS Airline president Jan Carlzon passed decision-making down to the *front line* of the company. He recognized that a ticket agent *was* the airline in the mind of a customer, and that every single interaction between a customer and any SAS employee was a *moment of truth*. To make that moment of truth a positive one for the customer, the employee had to be able to deal with the customer in a friendly, positive way. But, most importantly, the employee had to be able to solve the customer's problem on the spot, rather than kicking it upstairs to senior managers. In short, employees had to be empowered to act unilaterally—the very opposite of "hanging your brain on the gate."

"I've Left My Ticket at the Hotel"

One example he relates was of a passenger who arrived at the airport and discovered that he had left his ticket back at the hotel. Normally, when this happens, the airline simply tells the person that he will have to buy another ticket and send the other one back for a refund, a process that ties up the customer's money while he waits for that refund, which can take months in some cases. (In the U S, you are told that the process may take 90 days.) The SAS ticket agent looked at the schedule and said, "You have a couple of hours before flight time. How about we send a courier to your hotel to retrieve your ticket, and you wait comfortably in our lounge until it arrives?" And they did. Can you imagine the impact this action made on that passenger?

Teams at Volvo

Volvo is one company that has achieved very good results from the use of teams. Their president says, "I want every worker to say, 'I build cars.'" In most environments, a worker sees her job as menial and says something like, "I put lug nuts on wheels." There is a big difference.

> *"I build cars" is far more meaningful than "I put lug nuts on wheels!"*

In my interview with John Cashman (discussed in Chapter 1), I asked how much influence he had on the design of the plane. "Quite a bit," was his answer. He then told me about one such instance in which he was trying to convince Alan Mulally to design into the 777 a feature in which the rudder automatically compensates for loss of an engine during flight. When a plane has two wing-mounted engines, as does the 777, loss of an engine causes the plane to start turning (*yaw* is the technical term) to the right or left. If you lose a left engine, the right engine pushes the plane so that it tries to turn to the left. Only by adjusting the rudder can you keep the plane flying in a straight line.

Mulally was not convinced that this feature should be included in the 777, so Cashman put him in the copilot's seat of a 757 and took him up for a demonstration. Mulally has a pilot's license but is not rated for twin-engine jets. Nevertheless, Cashman told him to take the controls, but to put his feet on the floor and keep them there. (The rudder is controlled by foot pedals.) He then shut down an engine, and the plane went into a turn. Mulally had to get his feet off the floor and onto the pedals to correct for the engine loss, which takes some time to do. The reaction time could be extremely critical if you were to lose an engine at low altitude. Cashman then switched on the automatic compensation feature and shut down an engine again, but this time the plane corrected automatically. Mulally was convinced.

Cashman went on to say that, on the day of the first flight, assembly personnel were there to witness the flight of *their* airplane. They had been a part of the program from the very beginning, and they felt ownership for it. Had they not been made to feel part of the program, many of them would simply have said, "So what?" and slept late that day.

Certificates and Jackets

Patrick Shanahan was the first-line supervisor of a group that was to build the wing spars for the 777. He was relatively new to his job, but was well versed in engineering and quality. Alan Mulally had challenged manufacturing to attain levels of quality in the 777 that far exceeded what they had ever done before. He also established a recognition program for those who met or exceeded their goals. Tangible awards included jackets, T-shirts, and certificates for exceptional performance.

Pat's group delivered. They kept clear records of their quality, developed it into charts and graphs (the data sets us free), and applied for their awards. Pat asked them what they wanted. They were unanimous in their response—"We want Alan Mulally to sign our certificates." Pat promised to see what he could do.

However, when he asked the people administering the recognition program to have Alan sign the certificates, he was told that Alan was at too high a level and too busy to do so, and that the certificates would be signed by someone else. In due time, the certificates were signed and sent to Pat.

He then collected all of their charts and graphs, bundled them with the signed certificates, and dropped them off at Mulally's office. Within a day, they were returned to him. Mulally not only signed them himself, but he drew little airplanes on them and wrote personal notes to every person who received a certificate! But that wasn't all. He copied all of the certificates and sent the copies to Phil Condit, now CEO of all of Boeing, and Condit signed the copies and sent them to Shanahan's group.

Pat's people were blown away by this action on the part of Mulally and Condit. To them, these two had the status of "gods." The jackets and T-shirts were nice, because they signified to fellow employees who saw them wearing them that the recipients had performed exceptionally well. But they treasured the certificates more than anything. In fact many of them said that the certificate was going up over the mantel in their living rooms, so pleased were they that these two "giants" had taken time to honor them in this way.

Over and over, I am asked how to motivate people and how to reward them. And over and over, I tell people that it's simple—what people want is for their managers to appreciate what they do. There's nothing mysterious about it. But the appreciation does have to be genuine. You can't fake caring about people.

> *There's nothing mysterious about motivating people. One of the most motivating things you can do is let them know you appreciate what they do.*

No person can make good decisions in the absence of information.

SHARING INFORMATION

As I pointed out in Chapter 3, it has been common practice for many years for organizations to practice closed-book management. When I worked at ITT Telecommunications, the basic policy about information was that it was shared on a "need-to-know" basis. This practice certainly has some validity. There are sensitive financial facts that no enterprise would want to fall into the hands of its competitors—or even Wall Street. It may not be that the numbers signal the immediate demise of the company, but uninformed individuals might make that interpretation, so such information should be carefully guarded.

The only problem is that this practice gets carried too far. Managers learn that information is power, so they hug it to themselves. But they trap themselves when they do this. They often lament that their direct reports don't seem willing to take responsibility for anything. They pass all decisions to their managers to make, which places a heavy burden on the manager.

However, no person can make good decisions in the absence of information, and when managers hide facts and figures from their people, it is no wonder that the people won't stick their necks out by making decisions with severely limited information.

Some Benefits of Including Everyone

In a project management class in December 2000, I divided a class of thirty-eight people into six groups and assigned two principles to each group and had them list the benefits of their two principles. Most of these people have five to ten years of work experience, and a few of them had close to twenty, so they are seasoned people who can grasp the real-world benefits. Here are some of the things they listed for the "everyone-is-included" principle. As they are self-explanatory, I list them without comment:

- Promotes teamwork
- Achieves buy-in
- Develops shared responsibility
- Brings different perspectives to the table
- Makes work easier to delegate
- Brings out the "quiet ones"
- Develops individuals and groups

QUESTIONS TO ANSWER

- Who needs to be included?
- Are they included?
- What does inclusion mean? (Personal correspondence from Alan Mulally. Used by permission.)
- Is everyone included in *everything*? If not, from what are they excluded?
- Are they included all the time?

8

The Data Sets Us Free

It is easy to get upset about problems that exist in a project. But emotion doesn't solve problems. If you have data—facts rather than feelings—you can decide what to do to solve those problems.

It is easy to be paralyzed by the seeming hopelessness of a situation. Roz and Ben Zander recommend a practice to help us cope with bad situations. "It is *to be present to* the way things are, *including our feelings about* the way things are. This practice can help us clarify the next step that will take us in the direction we say we want to go" (Zander and Zander, 2000, p. 100).

Before continuing, however, it may be well to address the entire statement. The data sets us free. Free from what? My answer would be that the data sets us free from speculation, guessing, and needless anxiety. To quote Roz and Ben Zander

PRINCIPLE: The data sets you free.

again, "The practice of being with *the way things are* calls upon us to distinguish between our assumptions, our feelings, and the facts—that is, what has happened or what is happening.

> *The fact that someone didn't return your call is data. Why she didn't call is speculation until you know from her what happened.*

These are not easy distinctions to make considering the ongoing inventive power of perception" (Zander and Zander, 2000, p. 103).

As an example of this, when you call someone and leave a message and they don't call back, the only data you have is that the person didn't call you. And even that is speculation. She may have called and missed you and didn't leave a message. But for now, let's assume that she really didn't call you back. That is the data. Everything else is speculation—why she didn't call, for example. Her answering machine may have malfunctioned. She may not have checked her messages because she is unable to. She may be sick or on vacation or whatever. The only way to know what is going on is to get *more data*, which will set you free from guessing at what is happening.

Another factor that is important is that we get hung up on how things *should* be, rather than on how they actually are. She *should* have called you back. The project *should* be on schedule, and it probably *would* be, if we weren't dealing with a bunch of idiots! Notice how getting overly concerned with what "should be" results in the need to place blame? If someone weren't responsible, we would be where we should be, darn it!

The thing is, placing blame does nothing to change the situation, but does result in an escalating round of recriminations, accusations, and defensive maneuvering, none of which does anything to solve the problem.

> *Placing blame does nothing to change a situation or solve a problem—other than to perhaps make your relationship with the other person take a nosedive.*

Once you know what is really happening, you can respond appropriately. As long as you are guessing, you may take steps that only make matters worse. This happened to me once when I thought a team member was turned off in my project. He sat with his arms crossed over his chest, never said anything, and seemed unconcerned about the meeting. Later, during a break, he approached me and said, "I really think we're on the right track!" I couldn't believe it. He was with me all along, but I misinterpreted his "body language."

What I lacked was actual data. I was interpreting the evidence incorrectly. Had I taken time to ask him what he thought, I would have learned sooner that there was no problem.

Projects and organizations must be managed by the data. This also means, of course, that you must have metrics of performance, as I discussed in Chapter 5, which is something that many organizations lack. Furthermore, even when they have metrics, they have no systems for telling true status in every area.

If you don't know where you are, you can't be in control.

TRACKING PROJECTS

One of the difficult system issues we have to address in project management is acquiring project status information. Normally earned-value analysis is used to do this, but earned-value can be hard to apply to certain kinds of work. In developing software, for example, it can be very hard to tell if a module is actually complete. Yes, it works okay as a module, but when you link it to all the others, will it still continue to perform correctly? If not, then it is not really finished.

It is for this reason that some people think that trying to measure progress is a waste of time. My response is that you can't have control if you don't know where you are, and to me that is unacceptable. All you can do is recognize that the measures aren't as accurate as is possible when measuring length or weight, but they are better than nothing. The *tolerances* of the measures will simply be larger than you can obtain when measuring well-defined things.

Predicting the future is easy. It's knowing what's going on now that's difficult.

Another mistake commonly made is to measure schedule performance only. The progress reports then are prepared by running small bars inside the project schedule bars, to show how far along you are. An example is shown in Figure 8.1. This shows that task C is right on schedule.

However, let's assume that task C is writing software. The programmer (Sue) is telling us that she is right on schedule, but you

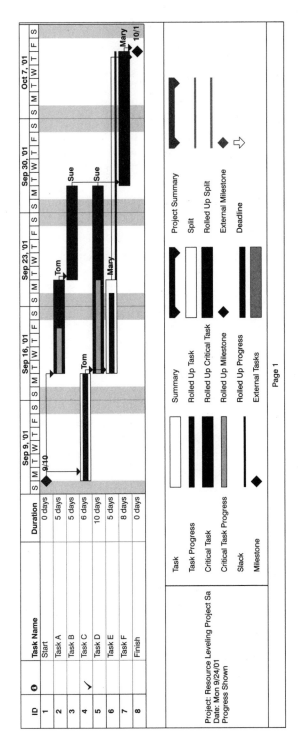

Figure 8.1
Progress report using a bar chart.

learn that she had estimated that her work would take 40 hours last week, and she actually had to put in nearly 80 hours to get the code written. Would you be concerned?

You should be. If her estimate was that far off, and she is continuing to write code for you in future weeks, then this may be an early sign of serious problems. You need to find out if this is a one-time problem or if it is expected to continue. If it is one-time, then you may be able to relax. Otherwise, if it is expected to be ongoing, you know that she will burn out eventually, so you had better take steps to correct for it right now.

The point is that if all you had been told was that she was on schedule, you would have no early warning that there is a problem, and you would have done nothing about it. The message, then, is that you must have an integrated cost-schedule tracking system if you are really going to know the true status of a project. This is commonly achieved with earned-value analysis.

What about Performance and Scope?

Be aware that there is a big assumption being made here, which is that performance and scope are okay. If her code does not work correctly, or if she has not really written as much as she thinks she has, then she is not on schedule. These two variables can actually be the most difficult to measure, but again, we have to try, or we cannot possibly have control of the project.

SOLVING PROBLEMS

The vice president of a large paper mill once told me about a project to rebuild a recovery boiler at the plant. These things are several stories tall, and are made of thick steel plate. The crane operator dropped one of the plates and bent it up so that it was unusable. Since they are custom-made, the vendor could not supply a replacement immediately. They were asked how long it would take to make one. Their best estimate was eight weeks. The people at the paper mill had heart failure! For every day that the mill was inoperative, it was costing them a million dollars in lost revenue. This eight-week delay was unacceptable.

The paper mill asked the vendor if they would allow them to send a scheduler over to help schedule making a new plate. They did. By working with the people in the boiler company, he was able to put together a schedule that allowed them to make a new plate in about three weeks. The savings more than paid for the expense of dedicating the scheduler to help the vendor.

You see, the vendor didn't have a well-defined process, and they were giving their best guess as to how long it would take—and it actually might have taken that long if they had worked according to normal procedures. But by putting together a good schedule, they cut the time by more than half.

This incident actually supports two of our principles. First, you've got to have a plan. Second, the data sets us free. The schedule provided the data that told everyone they could actually produce the plate in less time than everyone initially believed possible.

SEEING POSSIBILITIES

When the situation is very grave, it is easy to get discouraged and decide that there is no solution. In fact, as Roz and Ben Zander say, "Often, the person in the group who articulates the possible is dismissed as a dreamer or as a Pollyanna persisting in a simplistic 'glass half-full' kind of optimism. The naysayers pride themselves on their supposed

> *The people who see a glass as "half-empty" are the ones wedded to a fiction, for "emptiness" and "lack" are abstractions of the mind, whereas "half-full" is a measure of physical reality.*

realism. However, it is actually the people who see the glass as 'half-empty' who are the ones wedded to a fiction, for 'emptiness' and 'lack' . . . are abstractions of the mind, whereas 'half-full' is a measure of the physical reality under discussion. The so-called optimist, then, is the only one attending to real things, the only one

The optimist sees possibilities.

describing a substance that is actually in the glass" (Zander and Zander, 2000, pp. 109–110).

QUESTIONS TO ANSWER

- ❏ What is the critical data we need to move forward to accomplish our plan, to accomplish our goals, to accomplish our vision?
- ❏ Does our "data" set us free to move forward with confidence where the status is different from the plan?
- ❏ Is it the most useful data?
- ❏ Is everyone's data included?
- ❏ Is everyone looking at the data regularly? (Personal correspondence from Alan Mulally. Used by permission.)
- ❏ Are appropriate people acting on the data?
- ❏ Is the data being used to chastise people or to solve problems?

9

You Can't Manage a Secret

The origin of this principle is interesting. In a phone conversation, Sherry Mizuta related to me how it happened. During a regular weekly progress meeting for the 777 program, someone from one of the departments gave the status report. When the report was concluded, someone from another group said, "That's not the way we see it," and gave some contradictory testimony.

The presenter admitted that he had not fully disclosed a problem that his group was having, whereupon someone said, "You can't manage a secret! If you guys are going to keep secrets, we may as well all go home." And so was born a new principle.

A notorious example of keeping secrets was the announcement by the baggage handling design team—four days before the new Denver airport was scheduled to open—that they were 13 weeks behind schedule! It is hard to believe that they had not known this

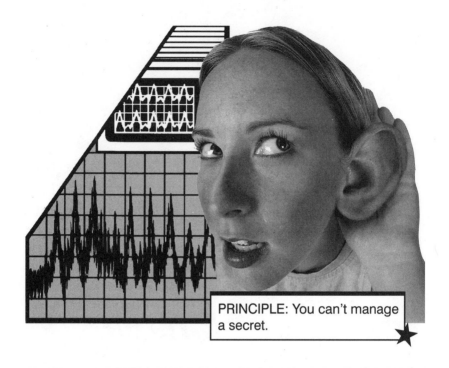

PRINCIPLE: You can't manage a secret. ★

for some time, and were probably hoping that they would solve their technical problems momentarily, but they held on to the secret until the very last minute, causing considerable embarrassment—and financial loss—to Denver.

People are often afraid to reveal problems in projects, because they think they will be trashed. And in many environments, this fear is well founded. However, it takes very little thinking to realize that you can't solve problems that you don't know about. Dr. Deming said—as one of his 14 points for performance improvement—that we should reward people for telling us about problems, rather than practicing a *shoot the messenger* response (Deming, 1986).

I was told once about a project manager who had to brief two army generals about the status of his project. He gave an honest report. There were a couple of problems, and he reported them and told what he was doing to correct them. The next day, he was relieved of his job. The generals had the macho idea that a project manager shouldn't have any problems. Now I ask you: How many project managers do you think will ever disclose any problems to those generals in the future? I'm sure you know the answer.

There are many factors that contribute to people being afraid to tell about problems. Engineers, in particular, are often reluctant to admit they are having a problem, because they have been schooled on the importance of being right. They also won't ask for help for the same reason. The result is that they spin their wheels trying to solve problems that could easily have been solved by other members of the team if only they had asked for help. Bell Labs found that this reluctance to ask for help was one factor that differentiated between engineers who were outstanding and those who were only average. The other factor was that the outstanding engineers networked within the company so that if they needed help they knew whom to call. This factor was considered so important that ATT created a training program to teach engineers how to network and ask for help when it was important (Kelley and Caplan, 1993).

ORGANIZATION CULTURE

In organizations that have a culture in which mistakes (or failures) are not tolerated, you can be sure no one will willingly tell that she has made an error or that what she has tried hasn't worked. The insanity of this can readily be seen if you consider innovation. The story goes that Edison was once asked if it were true that he had tried about 1800 things to make a lightbulb filament, none of which had worked, and he admitted that it was indeed true.

"Aren't you discouraged?" the person asked.

"No, I know 1800 things that I don't have to try," Edison replied.

Certainly, knowing what has already been tried and

If you aren't making any mistakes or having any failures, you probably aren't trying anything new.

didn't work is invaluable. Otherwise, you may wind up wasting a lot of time. Most importantly, if you aren't making any mistakes or having any failures, you are probably not trying much of anything new. We must differentiate between failures caused by stupidity and those caused by trying unproven things that contribute to knowledge.

Learning from Mistakes

It is one thing to make a mistake. It is quite another to repeat it. And this is almost certain to happen—not to the same person, but to other people—unless everyone knows about the mistake. By now I have asked several thousand people how many of them do regular lessons-learned reviews in their projects, and only about 5 percent of them raise their hands. Furthermore, even when they do such reviews, they sometimes hide the data from others, because they are embarrassed by it. Consequently, another team may make the same mistake made by the previous team, simply because they never heard about it.

In his book, *The Fifth Discipline,* Peter Senge discussed the importance of becoming a learning organization. Ten years after its publication, he was asked in a *Fast Company* magazine interview about his prognosis for whether companies can become learning organizations. His response: "It's possible, but highly unlikely." (May 1999)

Why such a glum outlook from Senge? Because there are many dynamics that prevent learning in organizations. It requires a change in culture—one that supports people, that encourages them to be honest, that responds to honest mistakes positively rather than negatively—in order to practice this principle. It also requires that individuals overcome their own conditioning of not being willing to admit mistakes or say that they are stumped by a problem. This may be the most difficult of all to achieve, because they find that even though their admissions are acceptable at work, they are still trashed everywhere else for such "flaws."

You can't quit now! I have millions invested in your education.

I once heard that a manager at IBM made an error that cost the company several million dollars. The next day, he tendered his resignation. His boss refused to accept it, saying, "I have millions of dollars invested in your education. You can't quit." What a refreshing, realistic response. It is safe to assume that this manager will never make that same mistake again, while a replacement may very well do so. This is one of the problems caused by high turnover in organizations. Those individuals who know what doesn't work take that knowledge with them, and their replacements, who do not know that something won't work, make the mistake all over again.

Some Examples of Good Practice

Managers are not the only ones concerned with being trashed for making mistakes. So are members of project teams—especially those projects that are very entrepreneurial in nature. MacMillan and McGrath, writing in the *London Financial Times,* discuss how managers should handle uncertainty. In any project that involves a lot of uncertainty (translate that into the word *risk*), "It is important for managers to help those involved in the project cope with uncertainty or they will find it hard to be decisive. Unfortunately, *it is now more expensive for companies to be slow than it is for them to be wrong . . .* the project manager should prevent employees from being overwhelmed by the complexities of the project. How? By setting a clear framework in which they can take action" (MacMillan and McGrath, 2000, p. 12, emphasis added).

This can be extended all the way to the factory floor. Paul Eisenstein relates an incident at Toyota's Georgetown, Kentucky, assembly plant as an example of not trashing employees because of problems. "Mike DaPrile, head of manufacturing . . . remembers clearly the day he thought he'd lost his job. He'd joined Toyota following a 25-year stint at GM. Soon after, he pulled the plug on the plant's assembly line. Water had gotten mixed with transmission fluid. . . . It took four hours to fix the problem, forcing Toyota to set new specs for the process. When the line started after half a shift was lost, DaPrile was called to see the plant manager.

"He stammered an apology, but his Japanese boss cut him off and said, 'This is a good day. You have learned.' DaPrile got a

It is now more expensive for companies to be slow than it is for them to be wrong.

promotion for his understanding of the Toyota system" (Eisenstein, 2000).

This is a good day. You have learned.

Describing the Toyota production system, or TPS, Eisenstein says, "Employees are an active part of TPS. 'You don't hide your mistakes,' DaPrile explained. If there's a problem, each team member is empowered to yank the so-called andon cord, bringing the line to a halt" (op cit.).

An Intolerance for Mistakes

I believe that the attitude some people have about sports explains why organizations have problems with people hiding mistakes. A friend of mine is a soccer coach for boys about twelve years old. She told me that the father of one of the kids was watching them practice one day, and his son made a mistake. His father began to berate him terribly in front of all the other boys. She called the father aside and asked him to lighten up. His response was indignant and totally macho. "He's got to win when he gets grown," argued the father. "He may as well learn now that mistakes aren't tolerated!" This problem is apparently widespread. I recently saw a copy of *Reader's Digest*, with a cover title: "How Parents are Ruining Kids' Sports."

Indeed, there is an attitude prevalent in the United States that teams must win at all costs. In fact, in most sports, a tie in the game is not allowed. Overtimes must be played so that there is a clear winner. Furthermore, at the end of the season, the second-ranked team may as well be ranked last. They are nobodies. Their loyal fans almost abandon them, so disgraceful is it for them to lose.

This attitude certainly carries over into business. We see businesses run in a take-no-prisoners fashion. The stockholders expect senior managers to do whatever is necessary to make the stock price increase, and if they don't perform, they are fired. The consequence is that many of those managers do stupid things to raise the stock price but destroy the company in the long run.

Please don't misunderstand. I am not antisports. I think there is great value in sports, but I believe *sportsmanship* is being lost. We have a lot of sore losers out there. We used to hear that it doesn't matter whether you win or lose, it's how you play the game that counts. This has been replaced by the opposite belief that it doesn't matter how you play the game, it's winning that counts.

We should welcome competition. When companies have no competition, they become complacent. A worthy competitor brings out the best in individuals and organizations alike.

THE ORGANIZATIONAL PERSPECTIVE

To return to the theme of organizations as systems, the reason this "no secrets" principle is so vitally important lies in the fact that everyone in the company is *interdependent*. We do not perform independently of other individuals or departments. This is true in general, but it is especially true in projects where there is a chain of actions, in which each successive one depends on the outcome of the previous action. If the deadline for the project remains fixed, as it usually does, and problems occur in a segment of the project, this means that succeeding tasks must be accelerated if the deadline is to be met. The earlier the warning given to those people at the far end of the chain, the better they can plan how they will accelerate their own work. If no warning is given until the handoff date is missed, it can be nearly impossible for them to respond appropriately.

EVALUATING MANAGERS (AND OTHERS)

People are encouraged to keep problems secret in a climate of blame and punishment. This is also true in an overly macho "can-do" culture, where people view missing deadlines or having problems as a failure on the part of the people involved. I mention in Chapter 10 on whining that allowing people to vent makes them more willing to admit mistakes or problems.

People are encouraged to keep secrets in a climate of blame and punishment.

You may also remember that when someone commented that nobody got trashed for admitting a problem in Mulally's review meeting, his response was that if he beat up on someone for having a red box showing status, then next week that person would just change the box to green without actually solving the problem. That is good common sense. (Of course, as Mark Twain remarked, "The trouble with common sense is that it isn't very common!")

You can be sure that nothing innovative will take place in a climate in which missing targets and having things go wrong is seen as a failure that must be punished, rather than an opportunity to learn. Although Deming advocated that we should drive the fear of failure out of our organizations, I'm afraid risk-averse corporate America by and large has ignored him. This is not true at Southwest Airlines.

As Kevin and Jackie Freiberg say, "At Southwest, it's okay to make mistakes—really! In 1985, after just three years with Southwest, Matt Buckley had moved from ramp and operations to manager of cargo at corporate headquarters. He proposed an idea that he was convinced would revolutionize the industry and catapult his career at the same time. The idea was a same-day, door-to-door cargo product called RUSH PLUS . . . Herb [Kelleher] . . . said, 'Let's try it!'" (Freiberg and Freiberg, 1996, p. 131). Unfortunately, it was a huge failure. "Buckley remembers, 'As far as I was concerned, my life was over and the headstone read, "Here Lies a Failure. RUSH PLUS Was Not Hot. Nor Was It Happenin'"'" (op cit., p. 132).

It was the most painful thing that had ever happened to Buckley. He was so humiliated and ashamed that he avoided people in the halls—especially Kelleher—and opted out of company functions. His depression was finally overcome when he realized that people were trying to help him heal. Later he said, "'Eating a little crow is good for the soul when you're in the right environment. RUSH PLUS was initially about me. It was about making my mark in my company. . . . Since then I've learned that's not what's rewarded around here. It's not about self. It's about the Golden Rule, and it's about serving rather than being served'" (op cit., p. 133).

Buckley has been promoted four times since RUSH PLUS. The reasons are simple. "First, the company values his entrepreneurial spirit and enthusiasm. Second, Buckley was able to turn failure into an opportunity for personal growth and maturity. If we are open to learning from them, mistakes teach us a lot about ourselves and the methods we use for getting things done" (op cit., p. 133).

Marvin Patterson (1993), former vice president for product development at Hewlett-Packard, says that managers should be evaluated on the quality of their decision-making process, not on the outcome itself. The reason is straightforward. Decisions are always made with inadequate information. If you had all the

> *If you had all the information you needed to make a good decision, it wouldn't be a decision.*

information you needed, it wouldn't be a decision; it would be a given fact. So you are always taking a risk when you make a decision—a risk that you have made the wrong choice.

Patterson draws on expected value theory to support his contention. The expected value of an outcome—over the long run—is the probability of the outcome multiplied by the payoff you will get. This is expressed as:

$$EV = P \times \$$$

where P is the probability of the outcome and $ is the payoff.

Now assume that you have an opportunity to enter into a business deal that has a probability of 0.9 of returning $100,000 on a given investment or expenditure. The expected value of the opportunity would be $90,000.

Your other option is to invest the same amount of money, but you have a 50 percent probability of returning $500,000. The expected value of this option is $250,000. Since the expected value of the second option is clearly much higher than that of the first choice, the second one is the one you should take.

The difficulty is that, with the 50 percent probability, you may very well come up empty-handed the first time you take that chance, and in many companies, you would never get a second chance. Knowing that, you can bet that most managers would choose option one, the 90 percent probability choice. Maybe they also believe the old maxim, "A bird in the hand is worth two in the bush," but you can bet it is the risk aversion of the organization that dictates the "sure thing," forgoing a chance at even greater returns.

As Patterson says, the manager who consistently went for the higher-risk options could be expected to do a better job for the company *over the long run*. Of course, we should also realize that, as is said about gambling, "Don't gamble if you can't afford to lose." If the company cannot possibly sustain the loss that might accrue from a high-risk choice, then it should certainly play it safe.

The point is that, if we evaluate everyone for taking chances and failing, they will *always* play it safe, and the company will grow old and content in its complacency.

QUESTIONS TO ANSWER

- We can't manage a secret. How is it really going?
- Does our data and our business plan review cover the key elements of our plan to accomplish our goals and vision?
- Does our data align throughout the enterprise globally?
- Is everyone on the same plan?

- ❏ Are people worried about issues that are not covered in our business plan review?
- ❏ Is it okay to really share the real status?
- ❏ Is it okay to be red?
- ❏ Will the team really help me if I am red? (Personal correspondence from Alan Mulally. Used by permission.)

10

Whining Is Okay . . . Occasionally

W hen people are really stressed out, they sometimes need a "shoulder to cry on." As Mulally says, "You can tell us if you need a hug, so long as whining doesn't become a habit. But let us know you're whining, or else we might believe that what you're saying is your plan" (personal communication).

Why in the world is giving people permission to whine a principle? I think there are a couple of reasons. In Chapter 4, I talked about arousing passion in people and showed that the words *motivate* and *emotion* have the same root. It is the emotion that people bring to work that makes them special. Machines are easy to deal with. They don't get angry, fall down on the floor and kick and scream, or have temper tantrums. But they are also totally sterile. Not much fun to be around.

PRINCIPLE: Whining is Okay—occasionally.

In other words, they don't have feelings. People do.

I also said that you can't expect people to leave their negative emotions outside and just bring in their positive side. It doesn't work that way. As Herzberg said, there are factors that motivate people and those that demotivate them. What is often overlooked is that, when something is demotivating a person, you must deal with that factor—remove or correct it—before any attempt to motivate the person will work. For example, when death takes a friend or relative, the individual who is feeling that loss can't be expected to have much enthusiasm for her job. Or, as happened to one of my technicians, when his wife walked out on him, he came to work the next day feeling absolutely bummed out. I sent him home with the advice that he talk to someone—his minister, a friend, or a counselor. He was too stressed to work.

You must remove factors that demotivate before trying to motivate someone.

So I think we must give people a chance to whine sometimes, so that they can unburden themselves and then get on with the job. Using the word *whine* validates the expression of negative feelings in an appropriate manner. I also notice that when people announce that they are going to whine, it immediately removes

124

some of the tension they were feeling. They lighten up a little. The situation may even become cause for some humor. As Charlie Brown (Peanuts) said, "No problem is so big or so complicated that it can't be run away from."

I also think that when we permit people to ask for a "hug," we convey something very positive to them—we're here for you. We'll help you, because you're important to us, and we'll see you through this thing, whatever it is. What better way to build a sense of community, of family, or of teamwork than this?

> *No problem is so big or so complicated that it can't be run away from.*

Contrast this practice with a culture in which a person is told to keep his whining to himself. What message does that convey? It seems clear to me that it says, "We don't care about you as a person. You're just a means to an end." This takes us back to the mechanistic or organic view of the enterprise that sees people as having no purposes of their own, and it dehumanizes the organization. It ignores everything we know about human beings and what they want from life.

SETTING LIMITS

There is a premise that I like which states that no behavior is good or bad in and of itself, it is the outcome that it generates that we judge good or bad. Allowing people to whine turns behavior that could cause very negative outcomes—demoralization of the team, for example—into something acceptable and gains some control of it by imposing a limit. You can whine—occasionally. You aren't allowed to do it all the time. Nobody wants to hear constant complaining.

You will also realize that the next practice is tied to this one. "Propose a plan, find a way," is really a corollary to this one. You can whine, but when you finish whining, we expect you to try to deal with the situation in a positive manner. There will be more on this in Chapter 11.

Recognizing the Limits of Our Control

There is a final reason why this principle is important. For a long time it has been popular to adopt a very macho, "can-do" approach to management. It is characterized by such expressions as, "There are no problems, only opportunities." The role model for this behavior is Admiral David G. Farragut who said, "Damn the torpedoes, full speed ahead."

You cannot, by ignoring a thing, make it go away.

In moderation, this practice or philosophy is fine. It frames the job of every person in an organization as that of problem solver. However, carried to the extreme, it can cause foolhardy, ostrichlike behavior, in which people bury their heads in the ground and ignore the perils that threaten to sink their ship. This is ignoring risks, and you cannot, by ignoring a thing, make it go away. The proper response is risk management, in which risks are identified, quantified, and then managed through the development of contingency plans.

The very macho "can-do" attitude assumes that every manager and employee has complete control over how they do their work.

The first myth of management is that it exists!
—Source unknown

It ignores the reality of the person as part of a larger system, in which *interaction* is the reality, not *unilateral action*. In systems theory, the Law of Requisite Variety says that in any system of humans or machines, the element with the greatest flexibility will control. Because there are limits to the flexibility any manager has, there are going to be times when you lose control. I think this "Working Together" principle is one way of acknowledging that this will happen, and that when it does, it will cause considerable frustration, and that it is okay to express that frustration.

It also helps to encourage people to practice the principle that you can't manage a secret (Chapter 9). If people are allowed to whine, knowing that nobody is going to shoot them for whining, then they are willing to bring problems to the table for discussion and solution, rather than hiding them.

So altogether, this principle fits nicely with the others. If you omit it from the set, you don't have a complete body of practice.

QUESTIONS TO ANSWER

- ❑ Is it okay to share my frustration? My disappointment? My concerns about the status? The future?
- ❑ Do I have a whine that really gets at the issue?
- ❑ Does my whine point fingers or blame others?
- ❑ Can I use our BPR data (plan and status) to put my whine in context of the plan?
- ❑ Am I showing my concern soon enough? Before we get further in trouble? With the people that can help the best? (Personal correspondence from Alan Mulally. Used by permission.)

11

Propose a Plan, Find a Way

*T*his principle is tied directly to the previous one, "Whining is okay—occasionally." Too often when people are faced with difficult situations, they feel like giving up. That is understandable. However, it won't lead to success.

We might call this the principle of persistence. Don't give up. Find a way to solve the problem. At the very least, hang in there.

I saw a living example of this one year when a female crow somehow broke her leg. She was hopping around on one leg, the other jutting out at a right angle from her body, it was so severely broken. My first thought was to borrow a shotgun and end her misery, but it soon became clear that she was carrying

> *I learned about persistence from a crow.*

129

PRINCIPLE: Propose a plan, find a way.

food to her chicks, and to kill her would be to pass a slow starvation sentence on them.

I don't know if they survived, but I believe they did. She persisted for weeks in carrying food to them, despite being in incredible pain. If crows were a nation of victims, to use Charles Sykes' (1992) term, she would have turned the children over to a welfare agency, claiming that she was disabled and could not care for them. Then she would have sat back and lived on a disability pension.

WHY YOU HAVE A JOB

I once read that the only reason any individual has a job is because the organization has a problem that he or she is supposed to solve for them. When, in the course of the job, a person gives up, he or she is abdicating the responsibility that has been entrusted to him or her by the organization.

When you have a problem, propose a solution. Don't dump problems on the team or the team leader to solve. If you do, then what is your job? If you need help, that's one thing, but your job is to first do everything you can to solve the problem yourself.

130

Clearly this is a principle that managers expect team members to follow, but it applies to project managers themselves. In other words, the project sponsor or other senior managers in the organization expect project managers to take complete charge of the project and be proactive in managing it.

This was a lesson I learned early in my career. My boss told me, "Don't dump problems on me. If you aren't certain that your idea is okay, tell me about it and I'll give you some guidance." He expected me to solve my own problems. If I needed to run the proposed solution by him, that was okay, but problem-dumping was not.

I also read a book early on that suggested the same for decision making. Make your own decisions. The author pointed out that you have as much authority as you are willing to *take*. If you wait for someone

> *You have as much authority as you are willing to take.*

to give you authority, it may never happen, because you haven't proved you can handle it.

About this same time, I knew a fellow who was fond of saying, "It's always easier to get forgiveness than permission." Together, these ideas really came together for me. My boss traveled a lot, and it

> *It is easier to get forgiveness than permission.*

would occasionally be a couple of weeks before I could see him. So I started making decisions and telling him about them at the first opportunity to meet. I am convinced that this practice resulted in my steady rise through the ranks to become chief engineer in seven years.

People in organizations are often reluctant to make decisions and propose solutions, in part because they have to be parented, schooled, and

> *Authoritarian practices lead to dependency in people.*

managed in a dependency mode. Authoritarian management and parenting lead to dependency in people. They learn to wait to be told what to do rather than taking initiative themselves.

I remember a man who worked in a company that was trying to implement self-directed work teams. The effort was foundering, and I was called in to help them make it work. During an interview with this fellow, he said, "I've been working here for twenty years. During that time, they expected me to hang my brain on the gate when I came in. Now they want me to carry the whole load." That is the most poignant expression of the dilemma that I have heard. All of a sudden, after twenty years, management decided they wanted him to take initiative, and he wasn't ready for it.

I believe that people in organizations relate to their managers in ways that are similar to how they interact with their parents. If their parents let them make their own mistakes, supported them, and encouraged them to be proactive, then they will do so with a manager who permits the same behavior. On the other hand, if they have been parented in a heavily authoritarian way, it can be very difficult to move them toward independence, but it is the only way a manager can get anything done. There is no choice.

TRUST REQUIRES RISK-TAKING

There are many reasons why managers do not encourage more independent thinking on the part of their followers, but one of them is fear. The manager is afraid that the employee will do something wrong, and as the saying goes, "The buck stops with me," so the manager tends to be a micromanager, always holding tight rein over direct reports or project team members.

The first rule of planning is that the people who must do the work should participate in planning it.

I knew one project manager who was doing all the scheduling for his team. That included estimating task durations. It was true that he had been doing the work for a long time, and did have some idea how long it would take, but I told him he was about to shoot himself in the foot. "If they can't finish a task in the time you have allowed," I said, "they are going to say, 'It's not our fault. We didn't think it could be done that fast anyway.'" And that is just what

Trust requires risk-taking.

happened. He was acting like the project czar, not the project manager.

The first rule of planning is that the people who must do the work should help plan it. I know that in large projects this is difficult to achieve, but I believe it is the only way to get real commitment to the plan. Remember the principle "Everyone is included"? They aren't included when someone does their planning for them.

When plans are made and "laid on people," you will find it impossible to get them to propose a plan or find a way when they encounter difficulty. They are inclined to say, "We did what you told us to do and it didn't work. But it was your plan, Mister, and we aren't responsible. If you want the problem solved, you tell us what to do!"

To illustrate how this works, consider parents of a teen-aged boy or girl who has just gotten that shiny new driver's license. What is the first thing the teenager wants to do when she gets home? Drive the car, of course–solo! The only thing her parents can do at that point is give her the keys and let her go. Otherwise, they will be hauling her around when she is forty years old, and that won't be fun for any of them. I am convinced that there are no atheists on that day. I don't care what they have professed to be-

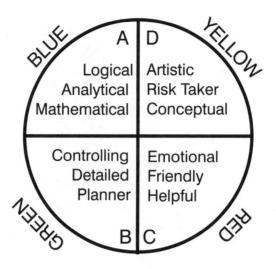

Figure 11.1
The Herrmann matrix.

lieve or not believe up to that time—this is a moment of truth, and all they can do is pray that she come back unharmed.

The point is that, if they never take a risk, they will never learn if she is trustworthy. The same is true of managers. If you want your people to propose a plan and take independent action to solve problems, you have to be willing to risk that they may not always do it exactly the way you would, and that they may occasionally make a mistake. Otherwise, you have a herd, not a team.

NOT EVERY TEAM MEMBER CAN DO THIS

Now I'm going to throw a bit of ice water on my very own pronouncements. Not every person can be expected to follow this principle. The reason has to do with thinking preferences. Ned Herrmann found that we have preferences for thinking in various ways. No doubt we have all heard about left-brained and right-brained thinking, but Ned went a step further and added another dimension. This leads to four different modes of thinking, as shown in Figure 11.1.

In quadrant A, people think in analytical ways, like number crunching and technical problems. Engineers and technicians usu-

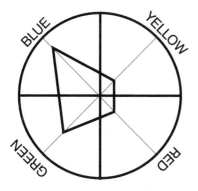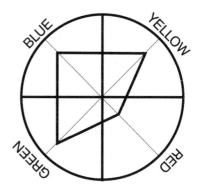

Figure 11.2
Some examples of profiles.

ally have strong preferences for this kind of thinking, as do financial analysts.

In quadrant B, the thinking is detail-oriented, organizing, and controlling. Accountants, tactical and logistical planners, and time managers have strong preferences for such thinking.

Quadrant C is oriented to interpersonal, musical, and spiritual thinking. Clearly people who are musically oriented, salespeople, and good group facilitators like to think in this mode.

Finally, quadrant D is holistic, conceptual, and artistic. Good strategic planning requires such thinking. So does doing product and architectural design and other such efforts.

By measuring the strength of a person's preference for thinking in each quadrant, Herrmann developed a profile that helps the person understand where he or she tends to gravitate. Examples of profile variations are shown in Figure 11.2. Note that they can be single-dominant, meaning that the person is oriented primarily to a single quadrant, or they can be double-, triple-, and quadruple-dominant. Ned believed that the ideal profile for a CEO was approximately square (quadruple-dominant), because a CEO must interact with people in all four modes, and must be able to understand and translate between them. I think the same is true for project managers, for the same reason.

Is it clear that a person with a very low preference for thinking in quadrant B is going to have trouble proposing a plan? They don't like doing detailed, organized thinking. However, it is very important to understand that the profile represents a person's *preferences,* not his or her abilities. Ned liked to say that each of us has a whole brain. However, it is true that preference leads to increased activity which leads to improved ability, so it does tend to be true that a low preference for thinking in a certain mode will be related to lack of skill in that area. So what we have to do as managers is coach and train these individuals to think better in the desired mode.

I have had several people in my teams who really had no idea how to do good work planning. Part of it was probably due to the thinking preferences that they had, but another possibility is that no one had ever taught them how to plan.

When I teach project management, my fundamental course walks everyone through constructing problem statements, clarifying objectives, developing project strategy, then working out the detailed implementation plan using work breakdown structures, critical path diagrams, and performing risk analysis. Not all of them enjoy some of this, but for many it is a revelation that shows them how to proceed with detailed planning in a methodical way.

The message here is that you shouldn't take for granted that every member of your team knows how to plan. After all, where would they have learned it? Very few schools teach planning, and even when they do, it is often somewhat superficial. You need to determine if a person's failure to follow this principle is due to her lack of skill in planning, or fear that she may be trashed if she is wrong (which makes her dependent). Perhaps she doesn't understand just what you mean when you tell her to propose a plan.

Leading people in a team is a lot like parenting. It requires coaching, encouraging, guiding, educating, and a lot of patience. If it is done right, you turn out some outstanding individuals.

QUESTIONS TO ANSWER

- ❑ So do we have an environment where it is not only okay to share the status and concerns . . . but expected . . . and expected to propose a go-forward plan?

❏ Large-scale systems integration, creation, and enunciation is about creating something out of nothing . . . there has to be a way . . . it is our job and mission and passion to find a way . . . so . . . we have an issue . . . we have a status off the plan . . . what is our plan? Our principle and practice is to find a way until there is no way, and then we will change the plan. We have so much talent and creativity to draw from. We trust that we will use all of our resources to get back on the plan. If not, there is no way for now. And we will develop another plan. But for now . . . get us started. Propose a plan. Ask for help with your plan. Move quickly. Show us the status next week. We will adapt. We will look for interdependencies. We all will help. We need your leadership because you are closest. We expect you to best know the status . . . and propose a plan to get back on plan. We need you. Boy, do we need your leadership to propose a plan. And thank you so much for your leadership to address your concern. (Personal correspondence from Alan Mulally. Used by permission.)

12

Listen to Each Other and Help Each Other

*I*n *Chapter 3 I discussed* the fact that we Americans have a love-hate relationship with teams. We tend to like working individually, and when we place people in teams, we find that they often don't perform well unless they are given specific training in how to be team players. Indeed, we tend to be super-competitive, both as individuals and as teams. We draw boundaries around our teams, our departments, and our companies, and by golly, no one from outside better cross that boundary!

Dimancescu (1992) has referred to these as *silos*, and we know that the walls of silos are very tall, so naturally people who live in a silo can be expected to have a very restricted view of the outside world. These silos restrict the flow of information—that vital "stuff" that is the "material" of knowledge workers. Most impor-

PRINCIPLE: Listen to each other and help each other.

tantly, they restrict cooperative effort, which is necessary to achieve anything really great.

You may remember the example of the scheduling exercise in Chapter 3. Groups had to plan a bank robbery, which involved picking the lock on the back door of the bank, and the question was when the alarm would sound—when they picked the lock or when they actually opened the door. In one of my classes, a fellow came to me and asked when the alarm sounded, and I suggested that he ask the expert, a woman in another group who was a bank vice president.

"Oh, can we ask her?" he said. "She's not in our group."

So even in a classroom setting, where there was no suggestion that groups were in competition, the silos had already been built and the competition had already begun.

What seems to escape many of us Americans is that competition and cooperation are opposite ends of a stick. You can't cooperate and compete at the same time. Listen to each other and help each other is about cooperation, which is the essential ingredient of team work and, as I have said, a necessity if you are going to achieve anything of any significance, like designing a 777 airplane or winning the Rose Bowl. Yes, the team is competing against another team, but *within* the team, there is cooperation.

You can't compete and cooperate with someone at the same time.

LEARNING TO LISTEN

I have been teaching team building for twenty years, and one of the things I always find is that most individuals don't know how to listen to others—or don't feel a need to do so—I'm not sure which. Alan Mulally is fond of saying that we have the illusion that when we talk to each other, communication has actually occurred, but this is often not the case. This is especially true when people become emotional about a topic. What you find is that each person in the discussion is thinking of what he or she will say when the other person quits talking (or sometimes people don't even wait—they simply interrupt). While people are thinking of a response, they are not listening to, and therefore not hearing, what the other person is saying.

Seek first to understand, then to be understood.

—Stephen Covey

I have had the experience several times as a manager of having to play the role of third-party mediator to employees who were in conflict. In listening to them argue, I became aware that they were actually saying the same thing, in slightly different ways, but because each of them was so passionate about making his or her

141

own point, no listening was taking place. One way to deal with this is to tell each person to repeat what the other person has just said. They can't do this without actually listening, and the practice forces them to do so, and they usually realize their common ground when they do.

The other point about communicating is that there is a big difference between *information* and *meaning*. Even when people hear what the other person said, they interpret it, so that the meaning intended by the person speaking is not the meaning received. That is why I like to say that the meaning of a communication is the response it gets. It makes no difference what you intended to convey. It is what the person perceived that will determine her response, so that, effectively, it is her own attributed meaning that counts.

> *The meaning of a communication is the response it gets.*

That then, leads to the next premise, which is that the responsibility for communicating rests with the communicator. This may seem to violate the principle, but until we have a world in which people have really learned to practice this principle—listen to each other—we will find ourselves having to take that responsibility. It is purely practical. I am communicating with the other person to achieve some kind of desired outcome. If the person does not get the meaning that I am trying to convey, then the desired outcome will not be achieved. That is my problem, and I must take responsibility for dealing with my own problems.

> *The responsibility for communicating rests with the communicator.*

Furthermore, I see it as a given that I can do nothing about anyone else's behavior, only my own, so I must communicate in a way that achieves the desired result.

As for members of the organization in general, however, if we can reinforce this principle, that they listen to each other and help each other, we may one day achieve true cooperation. Remember the comment by Roz and Ben Zander, that "transformation less by arguing cogently for something new than by generating active, ongoing practices that shift a culture's experience of the basis of reality" (Zander and Zander, 2000, p. 4).

So if we insist on the practice of these principles, what we hope to achieve over the long run is a change in the mode of interaction that typifies most organizations—a mode in which a lot of talking goes on but very little actual listening—to just the opposite.

One tenet that this principle translates into is that there are no side conversations allowed during meetings. If you need to talk, go outside. Talking while others are presenting is a sign of disrespect and should not be tolerated.

I would add that the same thing goes for cell phones. The abusive use of these wonderful devices has gotten out of hand. It was recently reported that Queen Elizabeth has banned them from the palace. It seems that members of her staff were getting calls while serving dinner and so on, so she banished them.

A woman told me that she was sitting in church one day, when a fellow in the congregation received a call. The minister was praying, but this fellow was undeterred. He kept right on talking.

Then I saw an article saying that this technology was so new that there are not yet any rules of conduct for it. Bullfeathers! My mother taught me not to talk in church—especially while the minister is praying, and she didn't have to revise her rule to include cell phones!

QUESTIONS TO ANSWER

- ❏ Do we have an environment and business plan review (BPR) where everyone is expected to listen and help each other?
- ❏ Are we seeking to understand before we seek to be understood?
- ❏ Does our BPR process and data have the leaders that need to lead actually leading and presenting and the leaders that need to really understand where we are listening and understanding? (Personal correspondence from Alan Mulally. Used by permission.)

13

Emotional Resilience

I remember my mother telling me, when I was very small, that I should always count to ten when something happened that I didn't like, rather than immediately flying off the handle. It's a good practice, but one that I never mastered. I'm afraid I fly off the handle and *then* count to ten. So, like Benjamin Franklin, who, near the end of his life, said that he had never mastered humility but he was still working on it, I also am still trying.

This is an important principle for managers to follow. Later I will share a practice with you that I have gotten from Roz and Ben Zander, whose book I have quoted a number of times throughout this book. It is called "being the board," and it is a practice that I believe offers hope to people like myself who have difficulty with emotional resilience. (The question I keep asking is, "Where were Roz and Ben thirty years ago?")

PRINCIPLE: Leaders must have emotional resilience.

KICKING AND SCREAMING

When problems crop up, the leader can't fall to the floor kicking and screaming. If she does, then people begin to think things are falling apart. Rather, she must maintain her composure and adopt a problem-solving stance. What are the facts (the data)? What do the facts tell us about the situation? What options do we have for dealing with it? What can be done to solve the problem?

I once knew a senior manager who had no tolerance for problems in a project. If the project manager admitted that there were problems, this manager would rant and rave and accuse the project manager of not doing his job properly. He managed by intimidation, and, indeed, most people were threatened by him. They soon learned to keep problems to themselves unless they were so severe that they could no longer be hidden. In other words, they learned to keep secrets, because the climate he created forced people to be self-protective by keeping problems to themselves.

In addition to making people keep secrets, however, his emotional response caused considerable anxiety in the people around him. Project managers would leave a meeting feeling stressed out, and some would pass their own stress down to their team members. It scared the daylights out of many of them, and some left the company rather than endure the ongoing emotional strain that it placed on them.

146

I often thought that, had he been measured on the negative fringe effects of his behavior—perhaps by subtracting the cost of turnover and other stress-related deficits in job performance of his people from his bottom line—then his performance numbers would not have looked as good as they did.

Most importantly, everyone lost respect for him. You can't be an effective leader when your "followers" don't respect you. You get compliance with your orders, at best, but you certainly don't bring out the best in people. In fact, you bring out the worst in them.

> *You can't be an effective leader when people don't respect you.*

BEING THE BOARD

Emotional resilience is not easy to achieve. It is especially difficult when you see other people or circumstances as the cause of your problems or when you are thinking in terms of *should*, rather than *what is*. It is important to understand, first of all, that no one can make you feel anything. Your feeling is your own response. It is a choice from many possibilities. You could laugh. You could cry.

> *No one can make you feel anything. Your feeling is a choice, and you can make a different one.*

You could say, "Isn't that interesting?" You could be angry. The choice is up to you. If you don't like the choices you have been making, make different ones. Following the principle *the data sets us free* certainly helps but may not carry you all the way.

Roz and Ben Zander suggest a practice that may help you deal with the emotions that tend to arise when a situation seems to offer no possibilities, when you are blocked, and when others refuse to cooperate. They call this practice *being the board*. The metaphor is to view your situation as a game being played, a game played on a board, and to see yourself as the board on which that game is being played. This allows you to move the conditions that cause the problem from the outside world inside the boundaries of yourself.

View your situation as a game being played.

The reason we refer to what is going on as a game is to make you realize that our accepted models for doing things come with an implicit set of rules. And "these rules govern our behavior just as surely as the rules of baseball govern the movements of the players on the field. When people play a game, they agree to a certain set of limitations to create a challenge . . . The purpose of describing, say, your professional life or your family traditions as a game is twofold. You instantly shift the context from one of survival to one of opportunity for growth. You also have the choice of imagining other games you might prefer to play . . . Naming your activities as a game breaks their hold on you and puts you in charge" (Zander and Zander, 2000, pp. 58–59).

We equate accountability with blame or blamelessness.

Ordinarily, we equate accountability with blame or blamelessness (op cit., p. 142). So when something goes wrong, we set about trying to figure out who caused the mess, so we can assign blame accordingly. And if we can't place blame on an individual, we may just blame the entire group. That's where these huge policy manuals come from—some individual did something unacceptable, and we re-

148

spond by blaming everyone and publishing a "thou-shalt-not" for them to follow in the future. Or, as my father used to tell my sister and me when neither of us would claim responsibility for something that went wrong, he would just have to punish both of us so he could be sure he got the culprit.

Blaming the other person for something that has gone wrong may satisfy our desire for self-justification but does nothing to solve the problem. Furthermore, it is helpful to realize that "there is nothing I

> *There is nothing I can do about your mistakes—only mine.*

can do about your mistakes—only about mine" (op cit., p. 142). Therefore, I take responsibility for whatever happens in my life. That does not mean that I caused my difficulties. It does mean that I control my *response* to what has happened. So "if I feel wronged, a loser, or a victim, I will tell myself that some assumption I have made is the source of my difficulty" (op cit., p. 143).

To illustrate how the "being the board" principle works, assume that you are involved in a car accident that was the fault of the other driver. From a strictly legal viewpoint, the other driver must take the blame. But your response might be to realize that any time you drive, you accept a risk. There is always risk that you may be involved in an accident any time you get into your car. Of course you could decide never to take that risk, but few of us would consider the life of a total hermit to be worth living.

Another example: When you build in a floodplain and a flood washes away your house, you can curse the river. But you must accept responsibility for your own decision to build where you did, knowing that the risk was there. Note that this practice is in direct opposition to the responses so many people now make to disasters. See, for example, Charles Sykes's book, *A Nation of Victims* (Sykes, 1992).

I will leave it to you to read more fully how to engage in this practice in the Zanders' book. But I would share with you one thought: "Imagine how profoundly trustworthy you would be to the people who work for you if they felt no problem could arise between you that you were not prepared to own. Imagine how much incentive they would have to cooperate if they knew they could count on you to clear the pathways for accomplishment" (Zander and Zander, 2000, pp. 158–159).

QUESTIONS TO ANSWER

- ❑ We are the leaders. It is our unique contribution and responsibility to lead . . . to have a plan . . . to know where we are . . . to have a plan to get back on plan. This can be scary when we are not on plan. We really don't know if we can get back on plan. Maybe the plan will not work for us. Maybe we will need a better plan.
- ❑ So . . . does everyone know and are they okay to deal with being off plan? That it is really okay to know. And we can't panic. Everyone is watching each other. If we give up or panic, everyone will panic. We are the leaders. We want to lead through the tough issues with focus and stability and inclusion. Our emotional resilience provides stability and hope for the entire team to propose a plan and find a way. If we don't demonstrate this behavior everyone will scatter . . . and we will not know if our plan needs to be changed or not. (Personal correspondence from Alan Mulally. Used by permission.)

14

Have Fun . . . Enjoy the Journey and Each Other

*W*ell, *I'm sure this principle* has already raised a few eyebrows. How can "Have fun . . ." possibly be a valid principle of managing complex organizations? Either those people at Boeing know something the rest of us don't know, or maybe we should sell our stock.

I hear you. Just hang in there, and I'll show you that the principle is valid. Really!

QUALITY OF WORK LIFE

In Chapter 3, Working Together, I discussed quality of work life and the fact that workers today demand more from the job than simply a paycheck. As was discussed in that chapter, when orga-

151

PRINCIPLE: Enjoy the journey and each other.

nizations were thought of as machines and then organisms, little thought was given to the purposes of workers. Then the Industrial Revolution led to the creation of work and workplaces that paid no attention to fun or learning on the part of workers. As Ackoff (1994) has pointed out, some of this thinking was part of the "Protestant work ethic," which sees work as necessary and necessarily unpleasant. When God cast Adam and Eve out of the Garden of Eden, he told them that henceforth they would have to earn a living by the sweat of their brows. Clearly, the idea is that work cannot be fun.

In fact, work was a punishment for the disobedience of God's command not to eat of the fruit of the tree of the knowledge of good and evil. Adam and Eve violated this commandment, and suddenly realized they were naked! "Oh my goodness. We can't let God see us like this! Quick, Eve, give me some fig leaves."

Adam and Eve may be the first buck-passers.

So God came along and noticed them wearing fig leaves, and asked, "Who told you that you were naked? Have you eaten of the fruit of that tree that I told you was forbidden?" Poor Adam.

Caught with nothing but fig leaves to hide behind. But he quickly invented a defense—Adam blamed Eve. "She gave me the fruit," he said.

Poor Eve was now on the carpet. So she blamed the snake. "He tempted me," she avowed. This may be the first recorded example of buck-passing, but it has been going on ever since.

"Why are our earnings so low?" asks the CEO in a challenging voice.

"Well, ma'am, it really has to do with manufacturing quality," explains the controller.

"What do you mean?"

"Their quality is really bad."

"Why is your quality so bad?" the CEO asks the manufacturing manager.

"It all has to do with purchasing, your majesty," the disoriented fellow replies. "They keep buying everything from the lowest bidder, and frankly it's junk."

"I resent that," says the purchasing manager. "It is not junk. It may be junque, but it is not junk."

"Quit playing with words," orders madam CEO. "What are you going to do about this?"

"Well, I'm going to find that darned snake," says the purchasing manager.

But back to Adam and Eve. Because they disobeyed Him, God threw them out of the garden, where up to now, every need they had was provided for. No more. Now God made them work for their living. As Genesis states, "You will have to earn your living by the sweat of the brow." So to this day, true believers know that if you don't sweat a little, you aren't doing real work, which is why knowledge work isn't *real* work. . . .

ENTER THE PROTESTANT WORK ETHIC

The Protestant work ethic asserts that the dissatisfaction that work causes should be accepted, if not welcomed, as an earthly purgatory in which sin is expiated by hard work and virtue is accumulated. So work is actually good for the soul. The greater the pain associated with it, the more it cleanses the soul. Which, of course, means that some jobs are better for the soul than others.

However, this is no longer the *prevailing* view of work, although I was told, early in my career, "Work's not supposed to be fun; that's why it's called work." And I have heard this said in recent years, so the view is still held by some. However, my guess is that this comes from individuals who have never been fortunate enough to do work that they found fulfilling.

> *Work's not supposed to be fun.*
> *That's why it's called work!*

To set the context for the discussion that follows, let us recall Ackoff's comments about quality of life: "The higher our standard of living, the more consideration we give to the fun we derive from what we do and its *meaningfulness*" (Ackoff, 1994, p. 71, emphasis added). Furthermore, this applies at all levels of a company, not just in the blue-collar workforce. To quote Ackoff again:

> *For example, the three owners and executives of a very successful but small hand-tool-manufacturing company wanted to diversify so they could become more involved in their business. Their company virtually ran itself, requiring little of their time or attention. Of course, they would like to have increased their profits, but not nearly as much as they wanted to increase the satisfaction they derived from running the business. This was a quality-of-work-life, not a standard-of-living, issue for the owners. The eventually added a new product line that required their intense involvement and their learning a whole new technology. They found the challenge exciting and their reinvolvement in the business a source of great personal satisfaction. All of this had an unexpected benefit: The morale and productivity of their employees increased because they saw their bosses working for a living (Ackoff, 1994, p. 74).*

BALANCING MIND, SPIRIT, AND BODY

In his best-selling book *The Seven Habits of Highly Effective People*, Stephen Covey (1990) tells a story about a person trying to cut

Balance mind, spirit and body.

down a large tree. A variation that I like better involves two people who are cutting wood. One of them works continuously through the day, stopping only for lunch. The other person stops frequently and disappears for a while. Those who are observing are certain that the person taking all those breaks will have less wood cut at the end of the day than the person who never takes any breaks. Of course, they are wrong. It is just the opposite.

How can this be? It's very simple. The person taking the breaks is sharpening his saw, so that when he is cutting wood, he is doing so very efficiently. The other individual, because he never takes any

How can he take all those breaks and still cut more wood than that other guy who didn't take any breaks?

breaks, eventually winds up with a dull saw that makes cutting wood slow going.

Deming (1986) told a similar story about a worker in a factory who ran a machine. For several years he ran that machine at full capacity. His output was phenomenal. Nobody had ever been able to get so much product from that machine. As a reward, the worker was promoted, and another person took over the job. Sure enough, as everyone had known, the new worker couldn't get nearly as much product from the machine as his predecessor. For one thing, the machine was always breaking down, and while it was being repaired, nothing was coming out of it.

As Deming pointed out, the previous worker had gotten a lot out of the machine in part because he never allowed the maintenance people to do any preventive maintenance on it. In short, he nearly destroyed the capability of the machine to produce.

Covey talks about the difference between production and production capability. He calls this P and PC. His premise is quite clear: You can't have high P unless you maintain PC. So he calls one of his seven habits the need to Sharpen the Saw.

He also calls for us to achieve some sort of balance between Body, Mind, and Spirit, adding a fourth category—social/emotional, which deals with service to society, empathy with each other, synergy, and intrinsic security (Covey, p. 288). It is this principle that I believe is being violated so pervasively in our society today.

OUR MOST VALUABLE RESOURCES

There is hardly a CEO anywhere in the world who doesn't proclaim that "People are our most valuable resources." In fact, "A 1995 national survey found that 98 percent of executives agreed that improving employee performance would significantly increase company productivity, and 73 percent claimed that employees were their company's most important asset. But when asked to rank business priorities, these same executives relegated investing in people to *fifth place* on a *six-item list*" (Rosen, 1996, p. 8, emphasis added).

> *People are our most valuable resources. Sure!*

> *Investing in people ranks next to last on a six-item list!*

This tendency is never more apparent than when the economy starts to get soft, as is true now, in January 2001, as I write this book. People are already beginning to talk about the possibility of a recession, and I know from past experience that this tends to create a self-fulfilling prophecy. My work in training is a perfect barometer of the economic climate. When managers get concerned about the economy, the first thing they begin to cut is training. I have been in the training business since 1981, and in every downturn, the first thing companies do is start canceling the training they have scheduled with me.

A number of writers have argued that this is exactly the opposite of what they should do (Deming, 1986; Peters, 1987). When business is extremely good, it is hard to take people away from jobs to have them trained because the company is already struggling to meet production quotas. In a recession, companies have excess capacity. If they were to invest in training during that time, they would increase their production capability, so that when the economy rebounds, they will be even better prepared than at present.

However, with our concern for short-term measures of organizational performance, this seems like insanity. When business drops, we need to take drastic steps to maintain profitability, and since sales are down, the only thing we can do is reduce costs, which generally means layoffs and reduction of all discretionary expenses—the most obvious of which is training that can be deferred.

Drucker (1973) and Rosen (1996) have both argued that our accounting system, as Rosen says, "[is] so sophisticated when it [comes] to finances and hard assets, but [is] downright primitive when it [comes] to measuring human assets" (op cit., p. 5). As he says, these accounting systems can't prove how different management methods affect human performance, and they definitely can't tell us how to maximize workers' creativity and commitment. I would add that the accounting system generally can't show the value of training, so that is why the United States usually ranks very near the bottom of the industrial nations in terms of its investment in training.

Countries like Australia and France have recognized the importance of investing in human resources, and several years ago started requiring companies to set aside a certain percentage of their revenues to invest in training their employees. It's too bad it has to be mandated, but it is definitely a step in the right direction.

Drucker argued in his book *Management: Tasks, Responsibilities, Practices* that we should be doing human resource accounting, and he argued this nearly thirty years ago. His argument has fallen on

People are the only truly renewable resource we have.

deaf ears. In my twenty years of consulting, I have not worked with a single company that did this.

The argument is flawless. We assign a value to capital equipment and depreciate it over time. We receive a tax advantage for doing so, which encourages companies to invest in such capital. But we don't realize that human "capital" does not depreciate. In fact, it is the only renewable resource we have, and it can be renewed to the point of senility, which would not occur nearly so soon if we did a better job renewing people.

Instead of renewing people, we burn them out. Then when they reach the age of maturity, where they can really contribute something of value to an organization, we force them into early retirement, because they cost too much money. We don't see them as an investment, but as an expense.

This is particularly appalling when it comes to engineers and programmers. It has been said that the half-life of such employees is about two to five years. What this means is that half the technology they learned in college is obsolete within two to five years after they leave school. As Figure 14.1 shows, the decline is exponential. If nothing is done to renew these individuals, the investment made by society and their em-

Engineers and programmers are going brain dead, even as we speak.

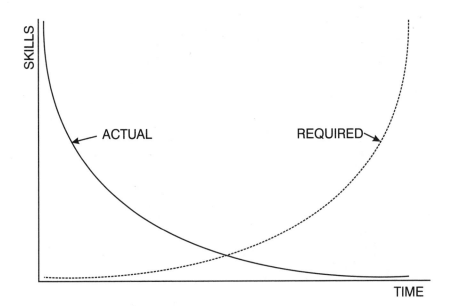

Figure 14.1
Decline of skills and increase in skill requirement over time.

ployer is wasted. Furthermore, as the figure indicates, the requirement for skills and knowledge is growing at an exponential rate, so that past the point where the curves intersect, the individual is becoming less and less valuable to the company.

The decay can be likened to depreciation of capital equipment, but whereas with capital we invest in preventive and required maintenance to "protect" our investment, deferring eventual "death" of the unit, with people we often don't make the investment, so we eventually lose that resource.

Now what does all of this have to do with having fun, the principle that is the subject of this chapter? It's simple. Having fun—at work or off the job—serves to renew the individual so that their production capability (PC) is maintained. If it were possible to assign an economic measure to this, I am certain that we would find a positive payback.

WATER COOLER TALK

One behavior of employees that absolutely drives some managers up the wall is what I call "water cooler talk"—those casual conver-

Lower-level needs must be met before a person turns to higher-level need fulfillment.

sations that people have on the job when, as the manager will tell you—they should be working, darn it! They aren't here to socialize. They're here to work.

There is no doubt that water cooler talk often goes too far and costs companies a lot of money. I have many times been appalled at how much talking some employees do on the job, clearly not doing nearly as much work as they should be doing. But like so many things, we tend to have a knee-jerk reaction to the bad, swing the pendulum all the way to the other side, and demand that there be *no* talking on the job that isn't work-related.

There are actually two outcomes of water cooler talk that benefit the organization, but which are seldom recognized. The first has to do with Maslow's hierarchy, which was discussed in Chapter 3. The three lower levels of the pyramid contain physical, security, and social needs. Human beings are social animals. We need contact with other humans. In fact, if we really want to punish prisoners, we place them in solitary confinement, to deprive them of human contact, thus depriving them of the fulfillment of this need.

In a country in which people spend at least one-third of their lives at work, as we do in the United States, the social interactions that take place on the job may be most of the social contact that a

Figure 14.2
Maslow and Herzberg compared.

person experiences during the day. Maslow believed that these lower-level needs must be met before a person turns to higher-level need fulfillment, which is where high job performance takes place. Herzberg talked about there being two factors to motivation. One factor was those things that actually give a person incentive to do something. He called these *motivators*. The other factor was needs that actually depress a person's motivation if they are not met. He called these *hygiene factors* and said that, while they don't provide individuals with motivation, they will depress motivation if not taken care of. Interestingly, Herzberg's hygiene factors correspond roughly to Maslow's lower three levels of his hierarchy. This is shown in Figure 14.2.

So what this means is that, if people are deprived of the opportunity to satisfy their social needs on the job, it will depress their motivation to do their actual work. For that reason, the principle that we should "have fun—enjoy the journey and each other" has a sound basis in motivational theory and practice.

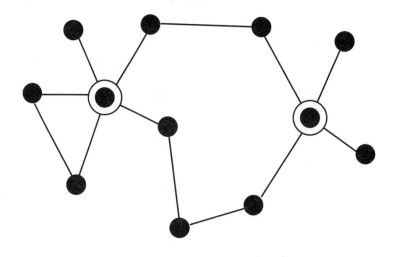

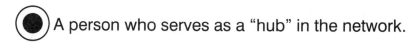
A person who serves as a "hub" in the network.

Figure 14.3
The informal network of an organization.

The second factor has to do with how things actually get done in organizations. Most companies have a *formal* organization chart that defines the reporting relationships that people have in the company. This chart tells us how work is *supposed* to get done. But it never tells the entire story. Studies by Dr. Karen Stephenson of the *informal* networks that exist in organizations have shown that these provide an extremely valuable service. It is through these informal networks that information flows, and this information is the "stuff" that knowledge workers must have to do their jobs well (Stephenson, 1999). She further found that certain individuals in these networks actually could be called "hubs," because much of the information that flows in an organization passes through these people. That is, they relay information out in all directions, as shown in Figure 14.3.

The formal organization chart almost never reflects the real

What is astonishing is that she has found that in companies that have a layoff, whether as part of a downsizing effort or for

162

some other reason, they sometimes lay off the hub individual and destroy the informal information network. The result is catastrophic. Without the normal flow of information provided through this individual, people can't make good decisions and otherwise do their jobs well. Naturally, the recommendation is to map an organization's informal network so that such inadvertent layoffs can be avoided.

The point of this is that water cooler talk is one of the modes by which information flows in the organization, and to insist that it be eliminated can have the same effect as laying off the hub person—the flow of information is stopped.

This can also occur when zealous managers decide that meetings are costing the company too much money and they order that all discretionary meetings be canceled and that attendance be reduced to those who absolutely need to be there. It also happens when travel is curtailed for budgetary reasons.

BUT CAN YOU MAKE MONEY AND STILL HAVE FUN?

There is always a party pooper out there! I know some of you are asking the old bottom-line question: Can you make money and still have fun? The answer is "absolutely," and "if your people aren't having fun, you probably aren't making as much money as you could be making." Want proof? Then read on.

"Since 1971, [the] eccentric and outlandish [Southwest Airlines] has established a consistent pattern of deviating from convention. When other airlines were creating big hubs, Southwest was flying point to point. Instead of serving expensive meals, flight attendants pass out nuts. Instead of wearing stuffy uniforms, they sport polo shirts and shorts" (Freiberg and Freiberg, 1996, p. 4). "The people of Southwest Airlines are radicals and revolutionaries—committed to the cause of keeping fares low to make air travel affordable for everyone. These people are scrupulous about working hard and zealous about having fun—so much so that many people want to know, 'Who *are* these nuts?' They are impassioned about treating each other like family. They hug, kiss, cry, and say, 'I love you' on the job" (op cit., p. 3).

Okay, okay, so the people at Southwest are nuts. But you still haven't answered the question—are they making money? Freiberg and Freiberg go on to say, "In an industry that is still reeling from the $12.8 billion loss it posted between 1990 and 1994, Southwest was the only airline to be profitable each year during that period . . . Southwest is the only U.S. airline to earn a profit every year since 1973. Its net profit margins—averaging over 5 percent since 1991—have been the highest in the industry" (op cit., p. 4).

Despite having the lowest fares in the business, they make more money and consistently grow—139 percent over the five-year period from about 1990 to 1995. That growth ranged from 8 to 36 percent annually. The also have "the most productive work force in the U.S. airline industry. The company services twice the number of passengers per employee of any other airline . . . [and] also gets more daily departures per gate and more productive hours out of an airplane than anyone else in the industry" (op cit., p. 7).

They also have one of the lowest turnover rates in the airline industry, approximately 6.4 percent per year. "Southwest people love working in an environment that encourages them to be themselves—even if they are nuts!" (op cit., p. 7). Considering the high cost of turnover, this alone helps make the airline profitable. I don't know what it costs an airline to replace a ticket agent or flight attendant, but I am sure it is more than the cost to replace a typical factory worker, and that figure runs around $6,000 to $10,000 in the southeastern United States. To replace a professional, such as a programmer or engineer, will cost a company $100,000 or more. Clearly, keeping employees is better than replacing them.

Southwest has also never furloughed anyone, except once in the early 1970s, when they experienced a cash crunch, and those *three* employees were immediately rehired. During the fuel crisis of 1979, the recession in 1982–1983, and the recession of 1990–1994, Southwest CEO Herb Kelleher "wouldn't even discuss the possibility of furloughing people: 'It never entered our minds. Our philosophy very simply is that it is a very short-term thing to do. If your focus is on the long term, the well-being of your business and its people, you don't do it'" (op cit., p. 7).

As for having fun, Richard Branson, CEO of Virgin, is the epitome of the philosophy in action. Says Jeffrey Garten, in *The Mind of the C.E.O.,* "Branson wants his employees to have fun, and he himself sets the example. He once appeared at a London event in drag to launch a new line of wedding gowns. He posed with nude models to announce his new cellular telephone business. He drove a tank down New York's Fifth Avenue to introduce Virgin Cola to the United States" (op cit., p. 116). He quotes Branson as saying, "'I think that too many chief executives sit in their ivory towers and plan things and forget that even the most stuffy-looking businessperson actually wants to enjoy himself, wants to let his hair down, wants to have a good time . . . If as chairman of the company I'm not having fun, I'm not going to want to take the trouble to get up in the morning and work really hard'" (Garten, 2001, pp. 116–117). By implication, neither will anyone else.

In short, the principle of having fun, which, at first glance, seems perhaps frivolous, has a very sound reason for being, supported by considerable research and practice.

QUESTIONS TO ANSWER

- Are we having fun?
- Why?
- Why not?

15

Final Thoughts

A*dopting these principles* means that you are effectively changing the culture of most organizations. Roz and Ben Zander, in their book *The Art of Possibility* (2000), say, "The history of transformational phenomena—the Internet, for example, or paradigm shifts in science, or the spread of a new religion—suggests that transformation happens less by arguing cogently for something new than by generating active, ongoing practices that shift a culture's experience of the basis for reality" (p. 4).

Ben goes on to say, "Although the practices we offer here are simple, they are not easy. I am reminded of a dispiriting moment in a cello lesson with my teacher, Mr. Herbert Withers. He was eighty-three years old, and I was eleven. I had tried to play a passage, but I couldn't make it work. I tried again and it didn't work, and a third time, and I was no more successful. I remember mak-

Managing for value becomes a mind-set that guides decision-making, planning, and resource-management.

ing a frustrated grimace and putting down my bow. The elderly Mr. Withers leaned over me and whispered, 'What? You've been practicing it for three minutes, and you *still* can't play it?'" (Zander and Zander, 2000, p. 5).

I believe you will find, as Ben Zander says, that these practices will take you far longer than three minutes to master, but I also believe that persistence will win out over the long run.

Alan Mulally begins every Business Plan Review meeting by rehearsing their principles. He does this ostensibly for the benefit of the visitors, who are usually Boeing employees (To my knowledge, I am the only outsider ever allowed to attend the BPR meeting). But the secondary objective is to drive these principles home in the minds of everyone—whether visitor or regular member of the group. It is through constant repetition and reinforcement that a change in culture is made. It is like running an advertisement—if you only do it one time, it will have almost no effect on your sales. But if you run it week after week, people begin to notice it, and the desired effect is achieved.

Furthermore, at the end of the meeting, Mulally reviews the principles again, talking about how important they are to everyone who is at the meeting, and how important they are to the success of the business.

The managers who belong to the leadership team then go back to their groups and do the same thing. They explain the principles. They reinforce them time after time, until people begin to understand that management is serious about them. This process instills the principles in everyone down through the ranks and eventually spreads the word to all employees.

No doubt there are skeptics within Boeing who do not believe that management is serious about the espoused principles, and I am sure there is some testing that takes place. This is where managers must be ever vigilant. If they backslide even one time and point fingers, exclude people, and so on, then the skeptic is confirmed in his or her doubts.

The fact is, we are all human, and even though we may believe in a principle, we don't always live up to it. When stressful events happen, we may not always be able to have emotional resilience. So I believe it is important to say this, to tell people that there may be occasions when a principle is violated, but that everyone should try to pick themselves up, dust off the momentary dirt, and try again. As the sports saying goes: no pain, no gain.

How long does it take? Mulally has been president of Commercial Airplanes for just over two years. At this point, it is clear that the leadership team believes in the principles. Without taking a survey of everyone in the entire company, I can't be sure how widespread the conviction is. But I am confident that continued reinforcement of the principles will eventually get most Boeing employees to believe in them.

THERE IS HOPE

I believe that practicing the principles outlined in this book may be the best way of moving people from the victim mentality to one of self-reliance and self-determination. I believe it because I am strongly convinced that the self-fulfilling prophecy is valid—you get from people what you expect of them. By treating people *as though* they are responsible, most of them will behave that way. Not all—there will always be some "casualties" who can't make the grade.But most will, and if you can get most of them to re-

You get from people what you expect of them.

spond, you will be doing your employees, yourself, and your organization a great service.

But I think the influence of these principles will be felt far beyond the boundaries of the organization. I believe they will extend to your suppliers and customers. And I believe that employees will take these principles home and practice them with their families and friends. Thus, you will have started a revolution in society, one that promises to reverse the trend toward victimization. This change in attitude will allow us to put into practice the admonition that we should think globally and act locally. By doing our part at the local level, the effect will be felt in all parts of the world.

CASUALTIES

It would be nice to think that the principles would "save" everyone, but they won't. In any cultural change, we know that probably 85 percent of all members will make the transition. But there will be some casualties. There will always be some people—at all levels in the company—whose mind-sets are so out of line with the new order and so resistant to change that they will not be able to change, and they may have to leave the organization, voluntarily or involuntarily. And there have been some casualties of the new order at Boeing, Southwest Airlines, and other companies that have tried to treat people well.

The analogy I like for this is that a tree with a diseased limb will eventually die if the diseased limb is not removed. Or, as the saying goes, one bad apple can spoil the entire barrel. It can be painful medicine, but it is necessary for the ultimate survival of the business.

THE NEED FOR LEADERSHIP

I have previously quoted Warren Bennis, who has said that we need more leaders and fewer managers. In his book, *The Mind of the CEO,* Jeffrey Garten quotes Bain & Company's Orit Gadiesh, who says, "'a leader who can provide a steady anchor is more critical than ever to the survival and success of a big organization. She calls this anchoring "true north," a combination of character and principle that makes it crystal clear what the leader—and by extension his organization—stands for'" (Garten, 2001, p. 113). Garten says that a good example of an executive with the "true north" approach is Richard Branson, Chairman of the $5 billion Virgin business empire.

It is clear that Branson believes in the principle that everyone is included, as well as having fun. Garten met Branson "in the trendy Royalton Hotel in New York, I in coat and tie, he in black denim jeans and short-sleeved shirt, and we sank into two comfortable chairs in the lobby for a long discussion" (op cit., pp. 114–115). Branson doesn't use the term "true north," but he practices it just the same. "'The core thing is absolutely and utterly the people who work for [a] company and if those people are proud of the company they work for, if they respect it and are listened to, the company will thrive'" Branson said. "'And so I think the number one, most important role for anybody running a company is finding the time for the people who are out on the front line making things work'" (op cit., p. 115).

Branson explained one of the ways he does this. "'Last night, when I came to New York, I was very tired,' he said. 'But I made absolutely sure that I took one hundred and fifty [of my employees] out—not to a formal dinner but to Mr. Chow's [so that we could] let our hair down, get drunk and have a good time. But I also sat down and listened and talked to them and made notes which I dealt with the next day'" (op cit., p. 115).

MODELS OF LEADERSHIP

It is outside the scope of this book to teach leadership, but I do want to make some recommendations. Kouzes and Posner (1987) conducted an extensive study of leadership and discovered a set of practices that effective leaders engage in. When these practices are combined with the situational leadership model of Hersey and Blanchard (1981), they are an excellent model for engaging in leadership. Remember, leadership is not a position, it is behavior. As Ben Zander says, "you can lead from any chair in the orchestra" (Zander and Zander, 2000).

If you want a living example of the Kouzes and Posner practices in action, rent a copy of the video *Stand and Deliver*. Watch it with the K&P practices in hand, and watch how Jaime Escalante engages in them. For those of you who may not know, Escalante was an engineer who left industry to teach math at Garfield High School in Los Angeles. In the first two years he was there, he took a group of some eighteen, mostly Latino kids, who began with a knowledge of mathematics barely up to understanding fractions, all the way to passing the advanced placement portion of the SAT test. Only about 2 percent of all high school students were taking the advanced placement test back then, and fewer passed.

In 1988, 88 of Escalante's students passed this same test, and in 1989 the number reached 109. Sadly, his methods violate most prevailing teaching paradigms, regardless of the fact that they clearly get results, and so he has left the school. Nevertheless, his approach to teaching is one of the best examples I know of leadership in action. Rent it. Watch it—several times. Then show it to everyone you know. We need leaders everywhere.

MULALLY'S THOUGHTS ABOUT THE PRINCIPLES

When he read the first draft of this book, Alan wrote a note to me in which he expressed his thoughts about the principles. He wrote them in a free-flowing style, which I am leaving intact as follows:

We probably contribute the most when we are safe and it is okay to learn and grow and be us . . . us the way we are now . . . knowing we will be different going forward.

Maybe this Working Together is about all of these things together. Working Together is about a culture we have embraced. Working Together is about principles we have embraced. Working Together is about practices we have embraced. Working Together is about expectations we have embraced. Working Together is about our environment we want to create. An environment where we can commit ourselves to working together to accomplish something we cannot do by ourselves. An environment where we are all safe . . . no jokes at each other's expense . . . no put downs. Only appreciation and help to learn and contribute and grow in effectiveness each year.

Maybe this Working Together is really about each of us. And maybe this Working Together is about how we feel when we are with another Working Together person. This Working Together is about opportunity for each of us. And maybe the Working Together is most about the tremendous personal responsibilities we accept and commit to a life-long process of growing to be the best Working Together person we can be . . . for ourselves and for everyone we will come in contact with. For me, this Working Together is the opportunity to contribute to something very special . . . to create value and meaning for so many people . . . to make a big difference . . . to feel the satisfaction, the true satisfaction that can only come from meaningful accomplishment . . . individually and as a team.

Have fun? You bet!

Enjoy the journey? You bet!

Enjoy each other? You bet!

Life is so precious and life is so fragile.

Working together provides us a framework for ourselves and others to live lives we can be so proud of. (Personal correspondence from Alan Mulally. Used by permission.)

Resources for Managers

*F*ollowing *is a list* of sources of information, books, and professional associations that may be helpful in managing.

CRM Learning: A good source of films for training, including *Mining Group Gold, The Abilene Paradox,* and many others. 2215 Faraday Avenue • Carlsbad, CA 92008 • Tel. (800) 421-0833

Jossey-Bass/Pfeiffer: A source of training programs, training materials, instruments, and books on management. 350 Sansome Street, 5th Floor• San Francisco, CA 94104 • Tel. (800) 274-4434 • FAX: (800) 569-0443 • www.pfeiffer.com

The Lewis Institute, Inc.: Founded by the author, the Institute provides training in project management, team building, and related courses. The core program is Project Management: Tools, Principles, Practices, and has been attended by over 20,000 managers worldwide. 302 Chestnut Mountain Dr. • Vinton, VA 24179 • Tel. (540) 345-7850 • FAX: (540) 345-7844 •e-mail: jlewis@lewisinstitute.com • www.lewisinstitute.com

McGraw-Hill Books: Source for other titles on project management. www.mcgraw-hill.com.

MindWare: The store for the other 90 percent of your brain. A source of tools, books, and other materials for helping enhance learning and creativity in organizations. They have a nice catalog listing their materials. 121 Fifth Ave. NW •New Brighton, MN 55112 • Tel. (800) 999-0398 • www.mindwareonline.com

Morasco, Vincent: A newspaper clipping service that operates on a pay-per-use basis. You pay only for the clippings you actually

175

make use of. A good source of up-to-the-minute information. Vincent Morasco • 3 Cedar Street • Batavia, NY 14020 • (716) 343-2544

PBS Home Video: Source of the video *21st Century Jet.* (800) 645-4727. www.shopPBS.com.

Pegasus Communications: Publishers of *The Systems Thinker,* a monthly newsletter. They also have videos by Russell Ackoff and Peter Senge, among others. P.O. Box 943 • Oxford, OH 45056-0943 • Tel. (800) 636-3796 • FAX: (905) 764-7983

Pimsleur International: The most effective way to learn a language on your own is with the cassettes using a method developed by Dr. Paul Pimsleur. Learning is virtually painless. 30 Monument Square, Suite 135 • Concord, MA 01742 • Tel. (800) 222-5860 • FAX: (508) 371-2935

Project Management Institute: The professional association for project managers. Over 60,000 members nationwide as of January 2001. They have local chapters in most major U.S. cities and a number of countries. 130 S. State Road • Upper Darby, PA 19082 • Tel. (610) 734-3330 • FAX: (610) 734-3266 • www.pmi.org

Project Manager Today: This monthly magazine is published in England, and has some good articles for the practicing PM. P.O. Box 55 • Wockingham •Berkshire RG40 4ZZ • England • Tel. (44) (0)118 976 1339 • FAX: (44) (0) 118 976 1944

Video Arts: A source for management training videos. Originally founded by John Cleese, many of them take a humorous approach to the subjects they cover. 8614 W. Catalpa Ave. • Chicago, IL 60656 • (800) 553-0091.

Web sites of interest:

www.joelbarker.com: Joel Barker's Web site
www.interact.com: Russell Ackoff
www.boeing.com: Obvious

References and Reading List

Ackoff, Russell. *Ackoff's Fables: Irreverent Reflections on Business and Bureaucracy*. New York: Wiley, 1991.

———. *The Art of Problem Solving*. New York: Wiley, 1978.

———. *Creating the Corporate Future*. New York: Wiley, 1981.

———. *The Democratic Corporation*. New York: Oxford University Press, 1994.

Adams, James L. *Conceptual Blockbusting: a Guide to Better Ideas, Second Edition*. New York: W.W. Norton, 1979.

Adams, John D. (Ed.). *Transforming Leadership: From Vision to Results*. Alexandria, VA: Miles River Press, 1986.

Ailes, Roger. *You Are the Message: Secrets of the Master Communicators*. Homewood, IL: Dow Jones-Irwin, 1988.

Albrecht, Karl. *The Northbound Train*. New York: AMACOM, 1994.

Archibald, R. D., and R. L. Villoria. *Network-based Management Systems (Pert/cpm)*. New York: Wiley, 1967.

Argyris, Chris. *Overcoming Organizational Defenses: Facilitating Organizational Learning*. Boston: Allyn and Bacon, 1990.

Axelrod, Robert. *The Evolution of Cooperation*. New York: Basic Books, 1984.

Barker, Joel A. *Future Edge*. New York: William Morrow, 1992.

———. *Wealth, Innovation & Diversity*. Videotape. Carlsbad, CA: CRM Learning, 2000.

Bauer, Eugene E. *Boeing: The First Century*. Enumclaw, WA: TABA Publishing, 2000.

Bedi, Hari. *Understanding the Asian Manager*. Singapore: Heinemann Asia, 1992.

Beer, Stafford. *Brain of the Firm* (2d Ed.). New York: Wiley, 1981.

Bennis, Warren G. *Managing the Dream: Reflections on Leadership and Change*. Cambridge, MA: Perseus, 2000.

Bennis, Warren G., and Burt Nanus. *Leaders: the Strategies for Taking Charge*. New York: Harper & Row, 1985.

Benveniste, Guy. *Mastering the Politics of Planning*. San Francisco: Jossey-Bass, 1989.

Barnhart, Robert K. *The Barnhart Concise Dictionary of Etymology: The Origins of American English Words*. New York: Harper Collins, 1995.

Blanchard, Benjamin S. *Engineering Organization and Management*. Englewood Cliffs, NJ: Prentice-Hall, 1976.

Blake, Robert, and Jane Mouton. *The Managerial Grid*. Houston: Gulf Publishing, 1964.

Block, Peter. *The Empowered Manager*, (2d ed.). San Francisco: Jossey-Bass, 2000.

Bodanis, David. *E-mc²: A Biography of the World's Most Famous Equation*. New York: Walker & Company, 2000.

Brooks, F. P. *The Mythical Man-Month: Essays on Software Engineering*. Reading, MA: Addison-Wesley, 1975.

Bunker, Barbara Benedict, and Billie T. Alban. *Large Group Interventions: Engaging the Whole System for Rapid Change*. San Francisco: Jossey-Bass, 1997.

Burns, James McGregor. *Leadership*. New York: Harper & Row, 1978.

Buzan, Tony. *The Mind Map Book*. New York: NAL/Dutton, 1996.

Carlzon, Jan. *Moments of Truth*. New York: Perennial, 1987.

Cialdini, Robert B. *Influence: The Power of Persuasion, Revised Edition*. New York: Quill, 1993.

Cleland, David I., and William R. King, Editors. *Project Management Handbook*. New York: Van Nostrand Reinhold, 1983.

Covey, Stephen. *The 7 Habits of Highly Effective People*. New York: Fireside Books, 1989.

de Bono, Edward. *New Think*. New York: Avon Books, 1971.

———. *Serious Creativity*. New York: Harper, 1992.

————. *Six Thinking Hats.* Boston: Little, Brown & Co., 1985.

Deming, Edwards. *Out of the Crisis.* Cambridge, Massachusetts: MIT, 1986.

Dimancescu, Dan. *The Seamless Enterprise. Making Cross Functional Management Work.* New York: Harper, 1992.

Downs, Alan. *Corporate Executions: The Ugly Truth About Layoffs—How Corporate Greed is Shattering Lives, Companies, and Communities.* New York: AMACOM, 1995.

Drucker, Peter F. *Management: Tasks, Responsibilities, Practices.* New York: Harper & Row, 1973, 1974.

Dyer, Wayne. *You'll See It When You Believe It.* New York: Avon Books, 1989.

Eisenstein, Paul A. "How Toyota's Kentucky Operations Mix People, Processes to Be Best." Investor's Business Daily, 12/4/2000.

Fleming, Q. W. *Cost/Schedule Control Systems Criteria.* Chicago: Probus, 1988.

Fleming, Quentin W., and Joel M. Koppelman. *Earned Value Project Management.* Upper Darbey, PA: Project Management Institute, 1996.

Fortune, Joyce, and Geoff Peters. *Learning from Failure: The Systems Approach.* Chichester, England: Wiley, 1998.

Frame, J. Davidson. *Managing Projects in Organizations.* San Francisco: Jossey-Bass, 1995.

Frankl, Viktor. *Man's Search for Meaning* (3d ed.). New York: Touchstone, 1984.

Freiberg, Kevin, and Jackie Freiberg. *Nuts! Southwest Airlines' Crazy Recipe for Business and Personal Success.* New York: Broadway Books, 1996.

Gardner, Howard. *Frames of Mind: The Theory of Multiple Intelligences.* New York: Basic Books, 1993.

Garten, Jeffrey E. *The Mind of the C.E.O.* New York: Basic Books, 2001.

Goldratt, Eliyahu M. *Critical Chain.* Great Barrington, MA: The North River Press, 1997.

Graham, Robert J., and Randall L. Englund. *Creating an Environment for Successful Projects.* San Francisco: Jossey-Bass, 1997.

Hammer, Michael, and James Champy. *Reengineering the Corporation.* New York: Harper Business, 1993.

Hancock, Graham. *Fingerprints of the Gods.* New York: Crown, 1995.

Harry, Mikel, and Richard Schroeder. *Six Sigma: The Breakthrough Management Strategy Revolutionizing the World's Top Corporations*. New York: Currency, 2000.

Harvey, Jerry B. *The Abilene Paradox: and Other Meditations on Management*. San Diego: University Associates, 1988.

Heller, Robert. *Achieving Excellence*. New York: DK Publishing, 1999.

Heller, Robert, and Tim Hindle. *Essential Manager's Manual*. New York: DK Publishing, 1998.

Herrmann, Ned. *The Creative Brain*. Lake Lure, NC: Brain Books, 1995.

———. *The Whole Brain Business Book*. New York: McGraw-Hill, 1996.

Hersey, Paul, and Kenneth Blanchard. *Management of Organizational Behavior: Utilizing Human Resources*, (4th ed.). Englewood Cliffs, NJ: Prentice-Hall, 1981.

Hiebeler, Robert, Thomas Kelly, and Charles Ketteman. *Best Practices: Building Your Business with Customer-Focused Solutions*. New York: Simon and Schuster, 1998.

Highsmith, III, James A. *Adaptive Software Development*. New York: Dorset House, 2000.

Ittner, Christopher D., and David F. Larckner. "A Bigger Yardstick for Company Performance." London: The Financial Times, 10/16/2000.

Janis, Irving, and Leon Mann. *Decision Making*. New York: The Free Press, 1977.

Jones, Russel A. *Self-Fulfilling Prophecies*. Hillsdale, NJ: Lawrence Erlbaum, 1977.

Kayser, Tom. *Mining Group Gold*. New York: McGraw-Hill, 1995.

Keane. *Productivity Management: Keane's Project Management Approach for Systems Development*, (2d ed.) Boston: Keane Associates (800-239-0296)

Keirsey, David. *Please Understand Me II*. Del Mar, CA: Prometheus Nemesis Book Company, 1998.

Kelley, Robert E., and Caplan, Janet. "How Bell Labs Creates Star Performers." *Harvard Business Review*, July 1993.

Kepner, Charles H., and Benjamin B. Tregoe. The Rational Manager. Princeton, NJ: Kepner-Tregoe, Inc., 1965.

Kerzner, Harold. *In Search of Excellence in Project Management*. New York: Van Nostrand, 1998.

————. *Project Management: A Systems Approach to Planning, Scheduling, and Controlling,* (5th ed.). New York: Van Nostrand, 1995.

Kiemele, Mark J., and Stephen R. Schmidt. *Basic Statistics. Tools for Continuous Improvement,* (3rd ed.). Colorado Springs, CO: Air Academy Press, 1993.

Knight, James A. *Value Based Management: Developing a Systematic Approach to Creating Shareholder Value.* New York: McGraw-Hill, 1998.

Knowles, Malcolm. *Self-Directed Learning.* New York: Association Press, 1975.

Koch, Richard. *The 80/20 Principle.* New York: Doubleday, 1998.

Kouzes, James M., and Barry Z. Posner. *The Leadership Challenge: How to Get Extraordinary Things Done in Organizations.* San Francisco: Jossey-Bass, 1987.

Kuhn, Thomas. *The Structure of Scientific Revolutions.* Chicago: University of Chicago Press, 1970.

Leider, Richard J. *Life Skills: Taking Charge of Your Personal and Professional Growth.* Paramus, NJ: Prentice Hall, 1994.

————. *The Power of Purpose: Creating Meaning in Your Life and Work.* San Francisco: Berrett Koehler, 1997.

Lerner, Michael. *The Politics of Meaning.* Reading, MA: Addison-Wesley, 1996.

Lewis, James. *Fundamentals of Project Management.* New York: AMACOM, 1993.

————. *Mastering Project Management.* New York: McGraw-Hill, 1998.

————. *Project Planning, Scheduling and Control,* (3rd ed.). New York: McGraw-Hill, 2001.

————. *The Project Manager's Desk Reference,* (2d ed.). New York: McGraw-Hill, 2000.

————. *Team-Based Project Management.* New York: AMACOM, 1997.

MacMillan, Ian C., and Rita Gunther McGrath. "Corporate Ventures: Maximising Gains." London: Financial Times, 10/16/2000.

Maidique, Modesto, and Billie Jo Zirger. *The New Product Learning Cycle.* Research Policy. (Cited in Peters, 1987).

Maier, Norman R. F. *Psychology in Industry.* Boston: Houghton Mifflin, 1955.

Maloney, Lawrence D. For the Love of Flying. *Design News,* Vol. 51, Number 5, March 4, 1996.

March, James, and Herbert Simon. *Organizations.* New York: Wiley, 1966.

Maslow, Abraham. *Motivation and Personality* (2d ed.). New York: Harper & Row, 1970.

McCartney, Scott. "Out of the Blue. How Two Pacific Nations Became Oceanic Aces of Air-Traffic Control." *The Wall Street Journal,* Friday, December 29, 2000.

McClelland, David. *Power: The Inner Experience.* New York: Halsted Press, 1975.

Michalko, Michael. *Thinkertoys.* Berkeley, CA: Ten Speed Press, 1995.

Miller, William C. *The Creative Edge: Fostering Innovation Where You Work.* Reading, MA: Addison-Wesley, 1986.

Mintzberg, Henry. *Mintzberg on Management.* New York: The Free Press, 1989.

Moder, Joseph J., Cecil R. Phillips, and Edward W. Davis. *Project Management with Cpm, Pert, and Precedence Diagraming,* (3d ed.). New York: Van Nostrand, 1983.

Mouzelis, N. P. "Bureaucracy." *The New Encyclopaedia Britannica.* 15th ed., Macropaedia 3 (1974).

Nadler, Gerald, and Shozo Hibino. *Breakthrough Thinking.* Rocklin, CA: Prima Publishing, 1990.

Nellore, Rajesh. "R&D Structures to Keep the Focus on Products." London: *Financial Times,* 12/11/2000.

von Oech, Roger. *A Whack on the Side of the Head.* New York: Warner, 1983.

———. *A Kick in the Seat of the Pants.* New York: Warner, 1986.

Packard, Vance. *The Pyramid Climbers.* New York: McGraw-Hill, 1962.

Pasmore, William. *Designing Effective Organizations: The Sociotechnical Systems Perspective.* New York: Wiley, 1988.

Patterson, Marvin. *Accelerating Innovation: Improving the Processes of Product Development.* New York: Van Nostrand Reinhold, 1993.

Peter, Lawrence J. *The Peter Principle.* New York: William Morrow & Co., 1969.

Peters, Tom. *Liberation Management.* New York: Knopf, 1992.

———. *Thriving on Chaos.* New York: Knopf, 1987.

———. "The WOW Project." *Fast Company Magazine,* May 1999.

Peters, Tom, and Bob Waterman. *In Search of Excellence.* New York: Harper & Row, 1982.

Pinto, Jeffrey K. *Power and Politics in Project Management.* Upper Darby, PA: Project Management Institute, 1996.

Pinto, Jeffrey K., ed. *The Project Management Institute Project Management Handbook.* San Francisco: Jossey-Bass, 1998.

Ray, M., & R. Myers. *Creativity in Business.* Garden City, NY: Doubleday, 1986.

Rickards, Tudor. *Problem Solving Through Creative Analysis.* Epping, Essex, England: Gower Press, 1975.

Rosen, Robert H. *Leading People: The 8 Proven Principles for Success in Business.* New York: Penguin Books, 1996.

Rosenthal, R., and L. Jacobson. *Pygmalion in the Classroom.* New York: Holt, Rinehart, and Winston, 1968.

Saaty, Thomas L. *Decision Making for Leaders.* Pittsburgh: RWS Publications, 1995.

Sabbagh, Karl. *Twenty-First Century Jet.* New York: Scribner, 1996.

Schuster, John P., Jill Carpenter, and Patricia Kane. *The Power of Open-Book Management.* New York: Wiley, 1996.

Senge, Peter. *The Fifth Discipline.* New York: Doubleday, 1990.

————. Interview in *Fast Company,* May 1999.

Smith, Hyrum W. *The 10 Natural Laws of Successful Time and Life Management.* New York: Warner Books, 1994.

Smith, Preston G., and Donald G. Reinertsen. *Developing Products in Half the Time.* New York: Van Nostrand, 1995.

Stacey, Ralph D. *Complexity and Creativity in Organizations.* San Francisco: Berrett-Koehler, 1996.

Steiner, Claude. *Scripts People Live By* (2d ed.). New York: Grove Weidenfeld, 1990.

Stephenson, Karen. *How to Analyze the DNA of Your Virtual Organization.* Paper presented at the Project Leadership Conference, Chlicago, Illinois, June 1999.

Sykes, Charles. *A Nation of Victims: The Decay of the American Character.* New York: St. Martin's Press, 1992.

————. *Dumbing Down Our Kids.* New York: St. Martin's Press, 1995.

Treacy, Michael, and Fred Wiersema. *The Discipline of Market Leaders.* Reading, MA: Addison-Wesley, 1995.

Vroom, Victor, and Arthur Jago. *The New Leadership.* Englewood Cliffs, NJ: 1988.

Vroom, Victor, and Phillip Yetton. *Leadership and Decision Making.* Pittsburgh: University of Pittsburgh Press, 1973.

Walpole, Ronald E. *Introduction to Statistics* (2d ed.). New York: Macmillan, 1974.

Watzlawick, Paul, John Weakland, and Richard Fisch. *Change: Principles of Problem Formulation and Problem Resolution.* New York: Norton, 1974.

Weisbord, Marvin. *Productive Workplaces.* San Francisco: Jossey Bass, 1987.

Weisbord, Marvin (ed.). *Discovering Common Ground: How Future Search Conferences Bring People Together to Achieve Breakthrough Innovation, Empowerment, Shared Vision, and Collaborative Action.* San Francisco: Berrett-Koehler, 1992.

Weisbord, Marvin, and Sandra Janoff. *Future Search: An Action Guide to Finding Common Ground in Organizations and Communities.* San Francisco: Berrett-Koehler, 1995.

Wheatley, Margaret. *Leadership and New Science.* San Francisco: Berrett-Koehler, 1992.

White, Gregory L. "In Order to Grow, GM Finds That the Order of the Day Is Cutbacks." *The Wall Street Journal,* Monday, December 18, 2000.

Wing, R. L. *The Tao of Power.* New York: Doubleday, 1986.

Wysocki, Robert K. *Effective Project Management* (2d ed.). New York: Wiley, 2000.

Wysocki, Robert K, and James P. Lewis. *The World-Class Project Manager.* Boston: Perseus Books, 2000.

Young, S. David, and Stephen F. O'Byrne. *EVA® and Value-Based Management.* New York: McGraw-Hill, 2001.

Zander, Rosamund Stone, and Benjamin Zander. *The Art of Possibility.* Boston: Harvard Business School Press, 2000.

Index

Note: **boldface** numbers indicate illustrations.

About the Author

*J*ames P. Lewis, Ph.D., is president of The Lewis Institute, Inc., a training and consulting company specializing in project management. Dr. Lewis has trained over 20,000 project managers since 1980 and continues to teach seminars for major corporations and universities throughout the United States, England, and the Far East. He has written articles for professional publications including *Training and Development Journal, Apparel Industry,* and *Transportation and Distribution,* and is the author of numerous books, including *Project Planning, Scheduling, and Control, The Project Manager's Desk Reference, Fundamentals of Project Management,* and others.

You can contact him at:

jlewis@lewisinstitute.com